Midwestern Tea Room Pleasures

By Joyce Decherd

Cover Design and Illustrations by Judy Harris
Typesetting by Douglas Decherd

Midwestern Tea Room Pleasures
by Joyce Decherd

For ordering information, write or call:
Joyce Decherd
P.O. Box 787
Moline, Il. 61626-0787
309-762-2652, (fax) 309-762-3158

First printing October, 1994
Second printing August, 1995
Copyright © 1994 by Joyce Decherd

All rights reserved. No part of this book may be reproduced or transmitted in any form or by any means, electrical or mechanical, including photocopying, recording or by any information storage or retrieval system, without written permission by the author except for the inclusion of quotations in a review.

Printed in the United States of America by:
G & R Publishing of Waverly, Iowa
ISBN-0-9642586-0-9

DEDICATION

This book is dedicated to my partner in life, work, and tea drinking, Douglas Decherd, with my love and admiration.

Thanks to the Lord who knows how to make a way when there seems to be no way—if we're willing to let Him.

A special thank you is extended to all the tea room owners and managers who took their time (our most precious commodity) to share their philosophies, dreams, and their fine recipes. You are my cup of tea.

INTRODUCTION

"How do you find these places?" my friend, Ricky, asked when I enthusiastically described recent jaunts to two Iowa tea rooms. I reviewed the highlights of my Iowa trip as I cruised home to central Illinois. I'd never given it a thought. Tea rooms were there. I went. A lot. I pondered her question, **"How do I find out about them**?"

My history as a tea room lover originated with a group of friends who took a fancy to old-fashioned indulgences such as homemade food and feeling pampered. A tea room opened in our town that supplied those basic needs, and we kept a sharp lookout for others. We weren't a pack of blue-haired floozies in lace aprons with big, plastic handbags and little fingers crooked in search of tea. We all had overloaded lives and liked to find places to escape for enjoyment of old-fashioned comforts. Looking for tea rooms was a serious business; and it wasn't unusual for us to cruise an hour or more to feast on memorable muffins, to sip tea, or to enjoy praiseworthy atmosphere and luncheon service.

One of the tea room non-floozies was Marie Wilhelm, a pooped potter, who wanted to evacuate the grueling craft show circuit. Pottery is heavy, bulky, breakable, and the most tedious ware to show. Aside from being an expert hauler of pottery, one of Marie's talents was "making memories." She liked to make special meals, decorate with homemade touches, etc., to create a memory scrapbook that would be treasured for years to come. She decided the tea room business was her cup of tea.

I was in the food service business as a manager for a large food service company and had no interest in joining her venture. My dream was to open a bed and breakfast home.

We started to search for a Victorian home for both businesses; the trick was to find commercially zoned property with adequate parking space. In a few months, we found a house that appeared to meet our needs.

I called a recommended contractor to inspect the property and advise us about renovation costs. Marie's and Steve's eyes locked that morning. Within three months, they were married and decided that working together in the thriving pottery business was a smarter choice than starting a tea room. Our plans were murdered by passion.

Five years later, I'm pleased to announce that Marie's wits have returned. She and Steve opened a gift store this year in the old Diekman's general store building on the main street of Denver, Iowa. The best news is that they saved floor space for Marie's tea room. Another dream has come true. (One to go!)

Tea rooms are well-kept secrets. The owners are busy with daily chores and few are marketing moguls. Advertising budgets are small. Customers usually discover tea rooms by word-of-mouth recommendations or in an advertisement in an antique or craft guide.

During my drive home to Illinois, I thought about my collection of bed and breakfast guidebooks which I used to plan vacations and get-away weekends. I knew that people who enjoyed bed and breakfasts, antiques, and crafts would also enjoy visiting tea rooms—if they could find them. A tea room guide could bring the masses out of darkness.

I hope this will be a helpful guide for locating the little jewels. No attempt has been made here to mention every tea room in the Midwest; this is merely a sampler of some of those offering outstanding service, food, or atmosphere.

New tea rooms continue to open at a rapid pace. Perhaps they'll be included in a future edition of this book. Readers' suggestions are welcomed. Phone ahead to check service hours at tea rooms because times are often adjusted seasonally, and reservations may be needed due to limited seating capacities.

The time has come to put on the tea kettle, break out the scones, and savor this sampler of midwestern tea rooms. Don't delay—so many tea rooms and (sigh) so little time!

ABOUT THE AUTHOR

I've always been intrigued by people who do interesting things. Writing this book was my chance to do something interesting. It was my opportunity to concentrate on a subject that's been dear to my heart for years and to promote the old-fashioned spirit of hospitality that fades as our modern lives accelerate to seemingly frantic paces.

A degree in Home Economics with an emphasis in Foods and Nutrition, experience as an interior designer, test kitchen home economist, caterer, and food service administrator have prepared me to understand some of the obstacles tea room owners face each day. However, I never cease to be amazed at their hard work, the risks they take, their accomplishments, and zest for pleasing their customers.

Writing this, my first book, has awakened a desire to recapture the essence of the rural midwestern life-style in which I was raised. I grew up in the country in Iowa where my parents farmed, raised livestock, milked cows, and had a huge garden with strawberry beds and sweet corn patches. We had our own apple trees and wild berry bushes. My mother preserved much of our food, sewed many of our clothes, and had time to crochet between baking homemade bread and desserts and making three meals a day. The neighboring farmers that helped my father "make hay" always knew they'd be fed well at our house. It was an old-fashioned lifestyle that has evaporated in less than one generation. Times were lean, but it all seemed so simple.

One of the main ways of entertaining in those days was by the preparation of grand meals to share with family and friends. Although food in tea rooms today is often more sophisticated than the fried chicken or pan-braised pot roast that my mother served her guests, many of the Sunday-best dishes will be recognized by those with backgrounds similar to mine. And the spirit of hospitality is much the same—a hearty welcome to a table laden with homemade treats.

Life is very different for me now. My husband, Doug, is an electrical contract designer—recently turned tea room book typesetter. We are also co-editors and publishers of the *Northern Illinois Country Register* newspaper. Recently, we moved from the Chicago suburbs to Moline, Illinois, where we hope to create some tea excitement and continue to visit tea rooms at every opportunity.

INTRODUCING THE ARTIST

Having been a tea room lover for many years and currently a free-lance graphic designer, infinitely qualified Judy Harris, of Judy Harris Designs, to be the artist and designer of this book.

When I met Judy, she was hoarding an inspired file of tea room drawings that she'd been working on for several years. She didn't know what she was going to do with the pictures, but the subject fascinated her.

Pinpourri is the name of Judy's jewelry designs. She's designed a collection of handmade pins with Victorian and seasonal motifs that are available in retail stores and in art shows in the Chicago area.

Judy received her Bachelor of Fine Arts degree at the Art Center College of Design in Pasadena, California. She has a wide variety of graphic arts experience including package design for major cosmetics and department store companies. She looks forward to illustrating more books (there are more inspired files about a variety of subjects).

Between her pilgrimages to tea rooms, she lives in the Chicago suburbs with her condo cat, Felicia, and can be found baking a myriad of tea time treats to share with her family and friends.

TABLE OF CONTENTS

What is a Tea Room? x

Illinois Tea Rooms
Cafe Las Bellas Artes 3
Cedar Pointe Tea Room 7
Country Thyme Tea Room 10
The Dicus House Bed & Breakfast 14
The Garden Room 19
The Jefferson Hill Tea Room 24
Lisa's Tea Treasures & Gift Parlour 29
Pinehill Bed & Breakfast 31
The Raspberry Tea Room 34
Seasons of Long Grove 38
The Spicery Tea Room 43
The Tea Party Cafe 47
Tiara Manor Tea Room 51
Windowpanes Tea Room 53

Indiana Tea Rooms
Almost Home 61
The Good Stuff 65
Queen Anne Inn 69
Rose Arbor Tea Room 74
Story Inn 79
The Tea Room 83
Trolley Tea Shop 88
The Victorian Guest House 93

Iowa Tea Rooms
The Barkley House Bed & Breakfast 99
Bette Dryer's Tea Room & Catering 102
The Blue Onion Tea Room 107

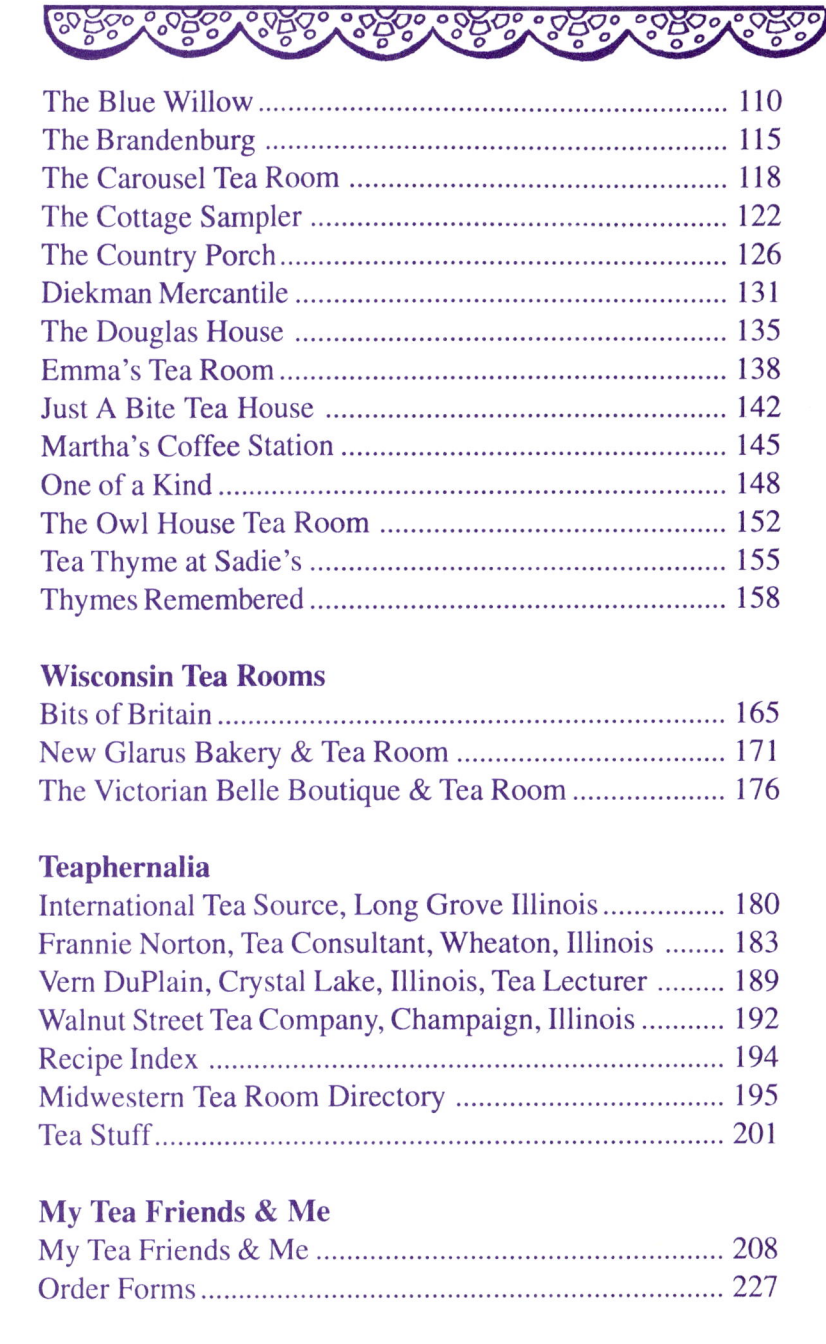

The Blue Willow	110
The Brandenburg	115
The Carousel Tea Room	118
The Cottage Sampler	122
The Country Porch	126
Diekman Mercantile	131
The Douglas House	135
Emma's Tea Room	138
Just A Bite Tea House	142
Martha's Coffee Station	145
One of a Kind	148
The Owl House Tea Room	152
Tea Thyme at Sadie's	155
Thymes Remembered	158

Wisconsin Tea Rooms

Bits of Britain	165
New Glarus Bakery & Tea Room	171
The Victorian Belle Boutique & Tea Room	176

Teaphernalia

International Tea Source, Long Grove Illinois	180
Frannie Norton, Tea Consultant, Wheaton, Illinois	183
Vern DuPlain, Crystal Lake, Illinois, Tea Lecturer	189
Walnut Street Tea Company, Champaign, Illinois	192
Recipe Index	194
Midwestern Tea Room Directory	195
Tea Stuff	201

My Tea Friends & Me

My Tea Friends & Me	208
Order Forms	227

WHAT IS A TEA ROOM?

"What **exactly** is a tea room?" If you don't know, don't be embarrassed—it's a question I've faced repeatedly. The question acts as a spur to my backside—increasing my zeal to cultivate potential tea room lovers and has encouraged me to attempt definition of a subject dear to my heart. However, after a year of travels and much research (scone sampling and tea sipping), I've only been able to draw generalizations. I can guarantee that a visit to a good tea room provides the feeling of being somewhere very special and will produce memories of being well cared for. There will be service of tea and other favorite beverages plus homemade, Sunday-best food. Beyond that point, the tea room tapestry begins to unravel; and the threads fray.

Midwestern tea rooms are often located in small (even tiny) towns, but metropolitan areas have their own versions. Tea rooms may be found in furniture stores, hotels, country clubs, department stores, chicken hatcheries, train depots, old store fronts, museums, art galleries, book stores, antique shops and malls, Victorian homes, or old farmhouses. Whenever I think I've compiled a complete list, additions become necessary.

The tea rooms may be divided into two general categories. In the Midwest, tea rooms are usually small, privately-owned restaurants that serve elegant, strictly homemade lunches with a belt-expanding selection of rich desserts. Other midwestern tea rooms specialize in the service of afternoon teas, providing a calm oasis for respite in a stress-filled world.

In either setting, tea room food is the essence of midwestern fare—fresh ingredients and few preparation shortcuts add up to a bonanza of the heartland's best. No franchise trucks roll in to deliver secret sauces and mixes, and no hints of fast-food are allowed. Tea room food is light because plenty of room must be saved for swoonful, sumptuous desserts.

The tea portion of the tea room experience is also varied. Besides being staunch drinkers of tea's major competitor, coffee, midwesterners are known to heartily indulge in two American contributions to tea drinking that cause disdain by some tea-buffs. In 1904, iced tea was invented at the Louisiana Purchase Exposition. During the same year, tea bags were introduced to the world by an American tea merchant who was looking for a way to send samples of his wares to customers. Some tea fanatics find neither iced tea nor tea bags equal to a fragrant pot of properly steeped tea. As a devoted tea imbiber, I prefer steeped tea using loose leaves because it seems more full-bodied and flavorful; but I'll admit that perhaps the extra fuss of preparation sways my opinion. As for those who stick their noses up at iced tea—I welcome them to endure a hot, humid, midwestern summer before they write their opinions in stone. Sometimes, nothing seems as refreshing as a tall glass of freshly-brewed iced tea.

The hospitality extended to tea room guests is the key. Tea room hosts expend much effort to make guests feel comfortable and pampered by attentive service in an atmosphere that is reminiscent of "gentler times."

This book will explore many of the midwestern variations of tea rooms. Perhaps **you** can decide **exactly** what a tea room is (or is it tearoom)? As for myself, I'm content to cozy up to a steaming pot of tea and reminisce about my last year of travels and of all the comforts midwestern tea rooms have to offer.

ILLINOIS

Illinois

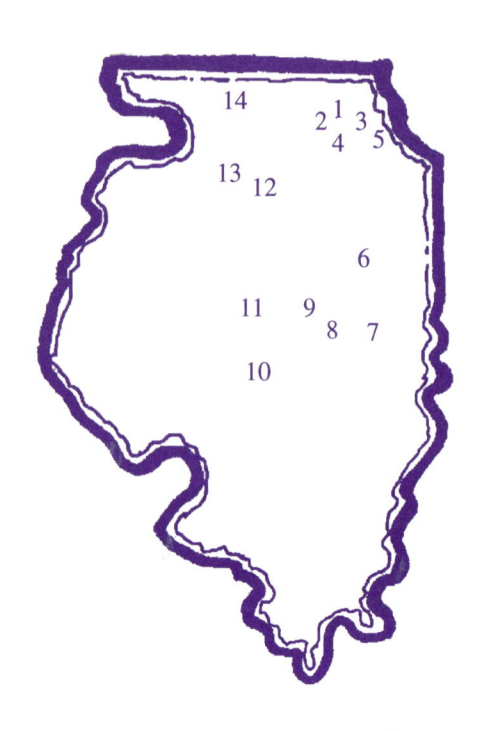

1. International Tea Source, Long Grove
1. Seasons of Long Grove, Long Grove
2. Tea Party Cafe, Geneva
3. Cafe Las Bellas Artes, Elmhurst
4. Jefferson Hill Tea Room, Naperville
5. Lisa's Tea Treasures & Gift Parlour, Winnetka
6. Country Thyme Tea Room, Paxton
7. Tiara Manor Tea Room, Paris
8. Windowpanes Tea Room in Inn on the Square, Oakland
9. The Spicery Tea Room, Tuscola
10. Cedar Point Tea Room, Pana
11. The Raspberry Room, Elwin
12. The Dicus House Bed & Breakfast, Streator
13. The Garden Room, Princeton
14. Pinehill Bed & Breakfast, Oregon

CAFE LAS BELLAS ARTES
ELMHURST, ILLINOIS

"You start by scrubbing floors, cleaning pots, and washing dishes. Then you stir the pot and move up the line from there. It's the old way of chefs' training," explained Gloria Duarte, owner of Cafe Las Bellas Artes, in the Chicago suburb of Elmhurst. Two years of rigorous training under other chefs, several stints as pastry chef in well-known Chicago restaurants, and Gloria was ready to open the only Mexican-European restaurant in the suburbs. Her restaurant is well known for its afternoon tea service.

Afternoon tea at Cafe Las Bellas Artes has evolved from the English style of tea service and includes, in my opinion, several items the English should take note of. The menu consists of scones, tea sandwiches, sweets, tea breads, coffee or tea, and a selection from the pastry menu. Because Gloria's love is pastry baking, you'll find the baked goods to be outstanding. Brioche is sometimes substituted for scones in the first course of the tea. Either are served with crocks of butter plus orange curd or strawberry preserves in glass apothecary jars. Both are made in Gloria's kitchen from fresh fruits. Chantilly cream, sweetened whipped cream with a bit of vanilla and whipped to soft peaks, is another special accompaniment.

The tea sandwiches differ widely from the little open-faced, crustless, white-bread, English version. Instead, they are served on Gloria's mini-croissants that are freshly baked each day. What a treat! They're an improvement in texture and flavor from the usual American croissants. One sandwich was filled with thin cucumber slices and the other with roast beef.

Tea breads may vary, but you can be assured you'll be served a sensational assortment. A typical sampling included a picturesque jumble of shortbread sticks, brownies with walnuts, Mexican wedding cakes, palmiers, and carrot-pineapple muffinettes. They are placed on a three-tiered plateau with the sandwiches, garnished with fresh berries, and delivered to your table by a waiter who takes pleasure in explaining the identity of each item.

After you think you've finished your feast, the waiter returns to take your dessert order! Caramel flan, strawberry tart with blackberry sauce and chantilly cream, hot fudge cake, bread pudding with Sandemann sauce—how could a dessert lover go wrong? If you feel adventurous, ask your server if the homemade cayenne ice cream is available (yes, you read right). It's one of the best selling desserts of the house and is Gloria's creation. She says it's more popular than chocolate, and it has "just that right zap" of flavor that customers love.

Afternoon tea is served with your choice of tea or coffee. Earl Grey is a mainstay; but flavored teas such as black currant or orange spice are also available, as well as plain black tea. Espresso or cappuccino may be substituted for a small additional charge.

Don't fret if you can't finish all your tea time treats. Portions are monumental, and the servers are happy to package leftovers to take home for later savoring. My tidbits reappeared from the kitchen disguised in a hand-sculpted, aluminum foil swan. Gloria says her staff is very creative and likes to develop ways to increase customers' enjoyment of afternoon tea.

Cafe Las Bellas Artes exudes a genteel, European flavor. You can gaze over the lacy half-curtains at the old-fashioned brick Elmhurst train depot and make believe you're in a land far away. Inside, the floor is a pattern of alternating black and white tiles. Vibrant, seasonal chintz tablecloths, deep cobalt blue stemware, and dramatic fresh flowers are eye-catchers.

The walls are a gallery of European, Mexican, and American art work. The paintings are for sale, but Gloria is content to leave them where they are. They and many of the antiques that line the glass-fronted Victorian piece from a French department store are overflow from Gloria's personal collection. "I can remember where I got each piece. We buy the things because we like them. Most of these things were in my home at one time," she said.

Elmhurst, Illinois

On frequent trips to Europe, Gloria and her husband look for English plateaus, tea pots, tea strainers, and china to use in the restaurant. They search for commercial service ware because of its durability. Mismatched china is used for teas because Gloria feels it makes tea time more interesting.

Michael Duarte, Gloria's son, is the restaurant's distinguished chef. His talents have provided Cafe Las Bellas Artes with the reputation as a fine place to enjoy breakfast, lunch, dinner, or Sunday brunch. Reservations are recommended for these meals as well as afternoon tea. Saturday afternoons can be especially busy with tea parties. "Tea is nicer than a luncheon sometimes, and it's plenty to eat," said Gloria. She said teas are becoming increasingly popular as a way to entertain.

Catering and gift baskets are two offshoots from the restaurant business. At holiday times, customers bring their own serving bowls for Gloria to fill with her special trifle.

Cafe Las Bellas Artes is just a chip-shot from the famed Oakbrook shopping center (perhaps a ten minute drive). Elmhurst College has been a landmark for years. The close proximity of the restaurant to the train makes the restaurant accessible from nearly any point in the Chicago area.

Admiring Cafe Las Bellas Artes is not a lonely experience. In 1993, the suburban area newspaper rated it as one of the top ten restaurants in the suburbs. It's a real find for tea lovers seeking a romantic atmosphere and generous portions of inspired treats at reasonable prices.

MEXICAN WEDDING CAKES

3 pounds butter
3 pounds 12 1/2 ounces flour
14 ounces powdered sugar
24 ounces ground pecans
vanilla, to taste

Soften butter, and mix with the rest of the ingredients. Form into walnut-sized balls. Place on ungreased cookie sheet, and bake in preheated 350° oven for about 15 minutes or until very lightly browned.

I have made similar cookies, but they don't compare to this recipe. Gloria said they are staples in her cafe because they are also one of her husband's favorites. The recipe is a large one—perhaps large enough for a wedding party!

CEDAR POINTE TEA ROOM
PANA, ILLINOIS

Cedar Pointe Tea Room serves copious quantities of two vital tea room ingredients: atmosphere and hospitality. Owners, Judy and Bill Clawson, are experts in the business of dishing out comfort—they've had lots of practice. They were foster parents for twenty years and have recently adopted two young sons. Judy says there is a 26 year age-span between their oldest and youngest children which leads me to believe the Clawsons are hospitable **and** ambitious.

"Our restored Victorian home with original tin ceilings, beautiful decor, dinner music, excellent food, and friendly staff are what our customers day they enjoy about their visits to Cedar Pointe," said Judy.

The old house is painted several shades of green; and there's a wrap-around porch gussied-up with white wicker furniture and a porch swing. There are tables and chairs for outdoor dining in nice weather. The exterior is rather plain, but visual treats await diners inside. The foyer door, with an oval etched-glass window, opens into a large entrance befitted with a claw-footed bath tub full of lacy pillows and dried flowers. A settee fashioned from an old bed is upholstered with rich brocade, and a scrapbook describing the history of the house rests on an old sideboard.

From the foyer, guests may view the jewel-toned, double dining rooms. Although rich, dark colors of forest green and cranberry are used to decorate, the appearance of the rooms is light and refreshing. Oak pedestal tables are covered with mauve tablecloths that are overlaid with crocheted doilies and sit on gleaming oak floors. The chairs are a comfortable mixture of rattan, antique, and bentwood styles. Cedar Pointe Tea Room has my vote as one of the most attractive tea rooms in central Illinois. It's easy to fritter away a relaxing hour or two while enjoying the atmosphere of this small town tea room.

Lisa Goatley, the Clawson's oldest daughter, manages the kitchen which looks like a residential kitchen with a few modifications. She offers a menu of standard sandwiches and salads but enhances the menu daily with special entrees and soups. She said the tea room provides her with the chance to experiment with recipes and to make favorites her husband won't eat at home. However, it's doubtful he complains about his wife's dessert repertoire. Heath Bar pie, pineapple cake, carrot cake, chocolate cream pie, and oatmeal pie were available on the day I visited. The chocolate and oatmeal pies are customer favorites. An entree favorite is the taco salad—hefted into a stand-up, edible, tortilla bowl. Food is served on green-tinted reproduction depression glass; testimony to the extent the Clawsons have concentrated on details that make the Cedar Pointe dining experience memorable.

Pana is located 45 minutes southeast of the Land of Lincoln historical sights in Springfield, Illinois, or just 20 minutes from Shelbyville Lake and its many marinas, beaches, boating, fishing, and golfing areas. St. Louis is only a 90 minute drive, and Pana is a pleasant change from big-city life.

You might find a treasure or two in one of the antique-filled rooms upstairs, and the Clawson's will welcome you with heartwarming hospitality. Everyone's going! They opened July 2, 1993, and within three months had visitors from 36 states and six foreign countries.

Pana, Illinois

OATMEAL PIE

3/4 cup white sugar
1/2 cup margarine
2 eggs, beaten
3/4 cup quick oatmeal
1/2 cup shredded coconut
3/4 cup dark corn syrup or dark brown sugar
1 teaspoon vanilla
1-9 inch pie shell, unbaked

Cream white sugar and margarine until light and creamy. Add beaten eggs, oatmeal, coconut, corn syrup, and vanilla; and mix until blended. Pour into pie shell. Bake at 350° for approximately 40 minutes or until firm.

Garnish with pecans and whipped cream, if desired.

"This recipe comes from a dear church friend and has been a favorite in our family for many years. It tastes like pecan pie." (The author says, "Amen!")

COUNTRY THYME TEA ROOM
PAXTON, ILLINOIS

People often ask how I discover tea rooms. The Country Thyme Tea Room in Paxton was an easy one. I just went to my mailbox and found a note from a friend in central Illinois who knew I'd be interested. My first stop there was just a teaser. Doug and I didn't have reservations, and we were on our way farther south into the center of the state. I don't know how it happened, but our car's nose just sort of veered off I-57; and there we were! Of course, the tea room was packed with fortunate customers with reservations and time to enjoy leisurely lunches. I had to be satisfied with a peek at the dining room. I saw just enough to know I wanted to see more and to say, "I shall return!"

Back in the car, I reported to my husband that the Country Thyme Tea Room looked suspiously like an Iowa tea room—lots of pink; Victorian, oak, replica chairs; crystal glassware; and I caught a glimpse of neat little baskets perched on some of the plates. And it was so full of customers. (I can't tell you how careful one must be in Iowa to insure oneself of a coveted dining space in many of its long-standing tea rooms.) Just talking about all this reinforced my plan to return soon. After all, Country Thyme was just an hour and a half from home—just a chip shot for a tea room jaunt.

Since I rarely meet anyone from Illinois who is familiar with Iowa tea rooms, my first question to Bonnie Kaeb had to be if she'd ventured over the Mississippi River lately. She said one of her hobbies was traveling to tea rooms all over Illinois and that she had lived very near Iowa at one time but had never been to any of the Iowa tea rooms. That blew my theory, but I was close.... osmosis perhaps?

Bonnie knows that it was God's perfect planning that got her into the business. Her son was ready to take over her previous farming duties, she'd been enjoying helping with her church's

Paxton, Illinois

catering and had entertained thoughts of owning a tea room of her own. When she was in Oregon visiting her sister, her husband read in a newspaper article that Diane Johnson of Paxton was opening a new gift shop called Fancies and Fantasies in the old skating rink and thought it would be nice if a tea room was added in the future. Bonnie thought it would be nice too. And wasn't her husband a peach to let her know about the opportunity? When her daughter-in-law, Shelly, said she'd be interested in helping, Bonnie couldn't have been more pleased. They opened in the Spring of 1995.

One of Bonnie's favorite ways to cook is with fresh herbs—hence the "thyme" in Country Thyme. Her menu is a mixture of beautifully presented salads with her special, homemade, herb dressings and entrees featuring pastas, crepes, chicken, beef, and pork. (The use of pork is unusual for a tea room but perfect in a central Illinois farming community where it has earned its reputation as "the other white meat.") A popular menu selection is their "Country Combination" which allows guests to have half a sandwich, a cup of soup or a small salad, and a taste of dessert. A whole barrage of desserts is a daily affair at Country Thyme. The long list is certain to include one of your all-time favorites. This is a perfect place to go to with an adventurous friend who will order differently from you. (Pledge an oath to share.)

At the time I visited with Bonnie, she and Shelly were able to cook all the food and serve their guests as a team. If you know anything about the food business and especially the tea room business, you'll admire their efforts and think about awarding them badges of tea room courage. Trust me. It's an amazing feat that takes a great deal of organization and energy. But after all, God has His hand in it, and He can do miracles. Bonnie said her only regret is that she and Shelly are so busy serving their guests that they don't get time to visit with their customers as much as they'd like.

Paxton is just one-half hour north of Champaign on I-57 or about an hour north of the Amish settlements in central Illinois. It's a little less than two hours south of the center of the Chicago suburbs and makes a perfect resting point for the southbound traveler. Central Illinois is full of wonderful sights, and Paxton is right on the way. Like many other small towns, Paxton is experiencing a sense of renewal and appreciation of its fine, old architecture. There are several antique and gift shops plus a couple of B&B's. It's fun to drive through the tree-lined streets and dream about the Victorian lifestyles that once inhabited the grand old residences.

Business has been brisk at the tea room. Even with such a short history, there is often a need to reserve your dining space. It's best to call ahead if you're driving from a distance.

In her life outside the tea room, Bonnie enjoys using her gifts of hospitality by helping her church prepare and coordinate meals for special needs, growing herbs and flowers, and enjoying life on the farm with her family. Her wish is to never lose focus of the truly important things in life.

Paxton, Illinois

RASPBERRY POPPY SEED DRESSING

1 1/4 cups sugar
2 teaspoons salt
3/4 cup herb vinegar
2 teaspoons dry mustard
2 teaspoons poppy seeds
1 pint cooking oil
raspberries, fresh or frozen

Place sugar, salt, vinegar, dry mustard, and poppy seeds in a food processor. Add oil very slowly and blend in until thick. Add raspberries until you get the color you desire.

FRENCH HERBED DRESSING

1/3 cup vinegar
1/4 cup lime juice
3/4 cup sugar
1 teaspoon salt
1 teaspoon dry mustard
1 teaspoon celery seed
1 teaspoon paprika
1 cup oil

Blend in food processor in the order given. Add oil very slowly as this will thicken the dressing.

THE DICUS HOUSE BED & BREAKFAST
STREATOR, ILLINOIS

Felicia Bucholtz said she was flat on her back after spinal surgery a few years ago—but it's hard for me to picture it. She's a wife, mother, full-time nurse, co-owner of a bed and breakfast, on the cookbook committee of the Illinois Bed and Breakfast Association, active in Streator and the Illinois and Michigan Canal National Heritage Corridor affairs, has a weekly radio show, as well as being a tea room hostess. I thought I was busy, but I'll reconsider.

I read about the Dicus House in a newsletter called Mary Mac's TeaTimes just in time for Doug and I to maximize our calorie intakes at their Victorian Sweetheart Tea.

Felicia and Art Bucholtz are the owners of this treasure trove of Queen Anne, 1890's architecture in Streator, Illinois (population 14,100). The home was inhabited for 90 years by the Dicus family until the Bucholtz family purchased it three years ago. They chose dramatic wallpapers and stately antique furnishings to complement the heavy, Eastlake-style woodwork. There are four lovely guest rooms, six marble fireplaces, and no remodeling has been done over the years to take away from the historic value of the home.

In 1993, Streator celebrated its quasquicentennial (125 years). Felicia, an ardent fan of Victorian customs, decided to contribute to the celebration by giving several Victorian teas. Later, people who had enjoyed the teas asked for more. Felicia hosted a fall tea and several teas during the Christmas season which were sell-outs. She enjoyed the teas so much that she's decided to have more of them. Art pitches in by helping with food preparation, service, and clean-up. "I'm a major part of the labor force," is how he tells it.

"I thought what I was doing was unique," said Felicia. "Then my sister gave me an article from the Chicago newspaper about places that were having afternoon teas. I found out about Mary

Streator, Illinois

Mac's newsletter in the article and contacted them for a subscription."

Felicia's teas are very special. They are unique because she did not pattern her service after any other modern tea parties. The Dicus House has a perfect floor plan for tea parties. The double dining rooms are large enough to each hold a large table with a service table between for tea time treats. She and Art bring silver platters to each table and, in turn, ask each guest to make his or her selections. Take my advice—don't select—try everything. It's all delicious; so eat yourself silly.

The Sweetheart Tea menu included tea sandwiches, cranberry scones with raspberry butter, and a battalion of sweets. (See a complete menu following this article.) Every bite is homemade, and it's likely you'll find something new to try because Felicia likes to modify recipes for interesting variations.

She served the Dicus House trademark chocolate-chocolate chip-peanut butter-oatmeal cookies at the Victorian Sweetheart Tea. All the favorite cookie flavors are rolled into one tasty batch of dough. I told Felicia about how my brother-in-law awakens in the early morning hours for a cookie snack. She told me that a lot of people do (You can relax, Kenny.); and that any hour of the night she is apt to hear the lid of the cookie jar clink in the upper hallway as guests help themselves.

Another interesting aspect of the afternoon, was the variety of teas that were served. Felicia invites guests to taste new kinds of teas. Our tastebuds were treated to Assam—a black tea, Blackberry—Felicia's personal favorite, and Jasmine Extra Fancy—a blend of oolong tea and jasmine flowers which had a heavy floral flavor. She brews loose tea leaves and sells small bags to guests who'd like to try their hands at authentic tea preparation at home.

Felicia, in Victorian costume and dramatic fashion, gave short lectures on the origin of the American valentine and wild women of the Victorian days. Art read a Victorian poem and received an encore. A short program is presented at each tea with intriguing names such as "The Romance Language of the Fan." Guests were provided with souvenir fans at that tea.

She sent valentine guests home with handmade valentines, gourmet chocolate coffee favors, and handmade herbal sachets after an extensive tour of their gorgeous home.

She told me her next projects are a Victorian bridal shower and to set up a calendar with a tea time schedule for the year. Art is the full-time curator/maintenance man at the Dicus House. He has many outdoor projects in the warm months such as painting the house and getting the grounds ready for future garden parties. An old wash house that looks like a little cottage sits adjacent to the mansion. Plans for it are uncertain, but it might become a gift shop or an extra bedroom. After seeing the results of their indoor projects, I'm certain the exterior will soon rival the home's elegant interior.

The Dicus House is about an hour and a half drive from the Chicago suburbs, is close to Joliet's attractions, and near three state parks. Murder mystery weekends are sometimes held at the bed and breakfast using themes from unsolved area crimes.

Art and Felicia are living their dreams, and their guests get to share the benefits of their inspirations with them. Don't miss the chance to participate in a tea, to reserve a romantic Dicus House guest room, or to rattle Felicia's cookie jar.

Streator, Illinois

VICTORIAN SWEETHEART TEA MENU

Salmon, Almond Chicken Salad and Cucumber Tea Sandwiches

Peanut Butter Chocolate Truffles
Chambord Truffles
Cranberry Walnut Cheesecake
Basic Chocolate Fudge Cake
Chocolate-Chocolate Chip-Peanut Butter Oatmeal Cookies

Assam Tea
Jasmine Extra Fancy Tea
Blackberry Tea
Mulled Apple Ginger Punch

PEANUT BUTTER CHOCOLATE TRUFFLES

1 cup peanut butter baking chips
3/4 cup margarine
1/2 cup cocoa powder
1-14 ounce can sweetened, condensed milk
1 tablespoon vanilla extract
Finely chopped nuts, unsweetened cocoa powder, graham cracker crumbs, or powdered sugar.

Over low heat, in a heavy saucepan, melt peanut butter chips and margarine. Stir in cocoa until mixture is smooth. Add condensed milk and vanilla. Cook for approximately four minutes, stirring constantly, until thickened and well blended. Remove from heat, and chill two hours or until firm enough to shape into one inch balls. Roll in nuts or one of the other suggested coatings. Chill until firm, approximately one hour. Store in the refrigerator in a covered container. Serve at room temperature for the best flavor.

ELEGANT BUT SIMPLE CHICKEN SALAD

2 cups cooked, diced chicken (light and dark meat)
1/2 cup mayonnaise
1/2 cup sliced almonds
Salt and pepper (to taste)

Mix all the above and chill. Butter bread for tea sandwiches.

Felicia says she always gets compliments from her tea guests about this easy recipe. It is wonderful on a small croissant.

THE GARDEN ROOM
PRINCETON, ILLINOIS

Chef Bonnie's back! She couldn't bear to stay away. Bonnie Cuffe had worked at the Strawberry Patch Tea Room in Princeton for fifteen years—first as a high school student and later as the owner. She was offered a chance to administrate a new convention center's food service in another Illinois town and decided to give it a try. However, she quickly learned she missed the individual contact she'd previously had with her customers. Soon she was back in Princeton, and was looking for a new tea room location with long-time co-worker and partner, Darlene Johnson. They opened December 16, 1991 in a flurry of activity with many Christmas parties to cater. "It was fun to be welcomed back to town in that kind of style," Bonnie said.

Discussion of the Garden Room must begin with a commentary on its food. One glance at the menu told me that the Garden Room was engineered by someone who'd risen from amateur ranks in the kitchen years ago. (Later, Bonnie told me she and Darlene have collective experience of over 25 years in the restaurant business.) All the tea room favorites were in place (quiches, salads, soup, etc.), but there were some other goodies such as Beef Stroganoff and meatball crepes, grilled lemon or Cajun chicken with pasta, and poached sole Florentine with a creamy spinach sauce and pasta. I side-stepped the mind-boggling array to try the Fumi chicken salad that had caught my eye on the outdoor menu board.

When I started writing this book, I was only familiar with basic chicken salad made with a blend of chicken, celery, mayonnaise, and if it was really fancy—the addition of grapes. Because it's bland and non-descript, I always wondered why people were mooning over this dish. Since the start of this project, I've experienced a total chicken salad conversion; and this one was totally different from all the others I've sampled. Chicken chunks, green pepper, cashews, toasted sesame seeds, and finely shredded cabbage were slathered with a tart, creamy, coleslaw dressing that would give a kick to anything it covered. (See the following recipes.) This was a dish worthy of company-best.

The menu promised the desserts to be "a poem of pleasure presented tableside." When the waitress brought the silver dessert tray, I thought God had opened the heavens and dropped the dessert angel down on a mission of good cheer. Talk about luscious! Six to ten desserts are offered each day. Bonnie said the three favorites are very simple recipes: coffee toffee cheesecake, orange Charlotte, and ice cream crunch dessert. On the day I visited, grasshopper pie made with mint flavor extracted from fresh mint leaves, strawberry plantation chiffon pie with pecans and pineapple, and a gooey pie with caramel, chocolate chips, and pecans were also waved in front of my face—along with my choice, a heavenly wedge of cheesecake spiked with amaretto flavoring on a cookie crumb and almond crust.

Bonnie said she feels the most unique feature of their tea room is their homemade food. Bonnie, Darlene, and their cooks use no frozen products. They prefer local dairy items and lots of fresh herbs. Soups and desserts are the two most habit-forming menu items.

"The realtor said there was no way to make this place 'country,'" said Bonnie. It was previously a black and purple cafe with flashing neon tube lights. He needs to take a second look. The garden theme is created by installing lattice-work over the ceiling. Lace curtains with a sunflower motif and lots of shutters shade customers from sun, much like a big front porch would. The room dividers are topped with flower boxes filled with philodendron tendrils, and colorful, folk art, staked, wooden vegetables pop out of the would-be garden. There are stuffed eggplant and tomato dolls and a watering can with silk flowers. Trimmed in dark watermelon green paint, the walls are covered with pastel, chintz-patterned wallpaper. The bases for clay garden

Princeton, Illinois

pots hold sugar packets. Country antiques provoke a homey atmosphere; and a cream and green enamel, woodburning cookstove is a family heirloom from a very special grandmother. It's settled in a corner on the old wooden floor, topped with a copper boiler which has been rigged with an internal hot plate for the service of their homemade soups. The hostess station is an old bakery case from the old Widmark bakery that was once in the tea room's historic building. Actor, Richard Widmark, worked in the bakery as a teenager.

Bonnie and Darlene maintain a large part-time staff to handle all of the catering services they offer. Recently, they catered a Victorian croquet party for nearly 300 guests.

Bonnie is one of Princeton's greatest fans. "Princeton is fantastic! The small town charm is wonderful. The shops are great. It all works together. Having a smaller dining room, I can mix with the customers. I'm into the individual contact thing." I don't think she's the only entrepreneur in Princeton with that attitude. Shop owners refer customers to each other and send customers down to lunch at the Garden Room. There's a spirit of camaraderie among merchants to promote themselves as a group.

The historic town is packed with specialty shops and antique stores. The ladies work with the owners of the Paper Horse gift shop to present occasional high tea luncheons. The Paper Horse is in an 1854 hardware store that is full of original appointments. It operated as a hardware store until 1986. Do not miss this marvel on your trip to Princeton. The owners will be happy to point out the many distinctive features and artifacts of the old structure.

Other points of interest in Princeton, about an hour from the Iowa border on Interstate 80, include the Lovejoy Homestead (an important Illinois Civil War underground railroad station), the huge Hornbaker perennial gardens, and Hoffman's Past Times Patterns (a famous source of replacements for vintage china, silver, and stemware). Each September, there's a Homestead Festival and

Pork Day for which Bonnie organizes a Homestead Festival Food Sampler program.

"I go for the non-mainstream places." She likes "relaxing, cute, laid-back places." If you're a tea room owner, don't be surprised if Bonnie introduces herself someday. Like the rest of us, she loves to go to tea rooms when she has time away from work. Could it be there is no cure for the love of tea rooms? I hope so.

FUMI CHICKEN SALAD

- 8 chicken breasts, cooked and diced
- 1 cup cashews
- 2 pounds cabbage, sliced very thinly
- 4 large green peppers, finely diced
- 1 1/2 cups mayonnaise
- 1 cup whipping cream
- 3/4 cup sugar
- 2 teaspoons salt
- 3 ounces sesame seeds, toasted

Toss the chicken, cashews, cabbage, and green peppers in a large bowl. In a small bowl, combine the mayonnaise, whipping cream, sugar, and salt. Add the dressing mixture to the chicken mixture. Finally, add the sesame seeds; and mix well. Refrigerate for several hours. Serve on lettuce leaves, and garnish with fresh fruit.

I left this recipe in large proportions. Once you taste it, you'll want to make a lot.

Princeton, Illinois

SNICKERS CHEESECAKE

3-8 ounce packages cream cheese
3/4 cup whipping cream
4 eggs
1/2 cup white sugar
1/4 cup brown sugar
10 ounces peanuts
unbaked cookie crust in 9-inch springform pan
12 ounces caramels, melted
1/2 cup whipping cream
6 ounces chocolate pieces

In a large mixing bowl, combine the cream cheese and 3/4 cup whipping cream. Mix well, and scrape down the bowl. Add the eggs, and mix only until incorporated (over-mixing at this point will cause your cheesecake to crack). Fold in the sugars and peanuts with a rubber spatula. Pour over the cookie crust in the springform pan. Bake for 1 hour in a preheated 350° oven. While still warm, spread with the melted caramels. In a small saucepot, bring the 1/2 cup whipping cream to a full boil; and add the chocolate pieces. Remove from heat, and stir until chocolate shines. Pour over the cheesecake; and refrigerate, uncovered, at least 6 hours or until cold.

Garnish with whipped cream and fresh mint leaves.

THE JEFFERSON HILL TEA ROOM
NAPERVILLE, ILLINOIS

It was a few days after Christmas, and I had allowed the post-holiday blues to settle deep into my bones. My husband, playing arm-chair psychologist, asked hesitantly—and I might add—gently, "Are there any tea rooms around here that you haven't visited yet?" He knows me so well. Within minutes, we were zipping off to nearby Naperville and the Jefferson Hill Tea Room. I was recovering from a sinus infection and still couldn't taste or smell; so I let my eyes and Doug be my guides on my maiden visit to this tea room. Both gave it a definite "thumbs-up," and my opinion has never wavered.

In 1845, a cottage-like, one-story, farmhouse was built that was destined to become the Jefferson Hill Tea Room. It was transformed in 1900, by the Kendall family, into the elegant Greek Revival mansion that it is today. A second story was added, and tall pillars and a fan window were added to the front. Mr. Kendall became the mayor of Naperville in 1917, and the home is still referred to as the Kendall home.

George and Shirley Olson purchased the mansion in 1971 as their residence and home for George's architectural business. The couple moved upstairs when Shirley opened a yarn shop. Next, a dress shop moved in; and a basement tea room opened in 1974, the brainchild of Shirley and her sister-in-law.

The first manager of the tea room was Jim Birkey, a young man who had traveled extensively. Jim encouraged the ladies to incorporate the tea room theme and had much influence on the menu selections—some of which are popular twenty years later.

In 1985 Kris and John Guill (the Olson's daughter and son-in-law) purchased the building and added a large addition that was designed by George. The addition, which enlarged the tea room floor plan and added space for more shops, received an award from the Northeast Illinois Chapter of The American Institute of

Naperville, Illinois

Architects. Several of the outer walls were left intact, and the old siding can be viewed from within. A three story atrium helps add light to the tea room (still located in the basement), but the building retained the character of a classic Victorian home.

Kris said that a lady from England once visited the tea room and asked to see the owner. She told Kris that Jefferson Hill Tea Room is just like the tea rooms back home. It's decorated in a very feminine manner, with shell-pink walls and white iron garden furniture. Many Victorian prints accent the walls, and a long, curved stairway connects the tea room to the upstairs shops. The Pantry, a shop in the tea room, is a good place to find specialty cookbooks, gourmet coffees, teas, latte, and tea accoutrements. There's a total of eleven specialty shops in the old mansion.

You'll find the servers to be a very hospitable bunch, and they even answer questions about ingredients or can make recommendations if you need to limit calories or fat intake. The food is stunning, thoughtfully arranged on the plate, and wins a "ten" in the food presentation category. It's fun to watch customers' faces of approval as they view their plates. The open-faced tea sandwiches are a customer favorite and may be ordered with meat and cheese fillings or with fresh fruit and cream cheese on cinnamon bread. Other popular entrees include: a rotating quiche selection, a ramekin of shrimp cheese spread with a warmed French roll, or beautifully arranged vegetable or fruit salads featuring the tea room's signature dressings. Men will enjoy a croissant sandwich or a filling on the marble rye bread that is always available, and no one will be able to say there's nothing appealing on the dessert menu. The flourless chocolate cake is Kris's contribution to the dessert menu and is a dense, fudgy treat. Two other favorites are the caramel apple granny and Skoog pie which is sprayed with edible gold dust. Both desserts are made for Jefferson Hill by outside bakeries.

If you miss the lunch hour, you'll be able to squelch pesky hunger pangs with the tea room's dessert and tea menu. Afternoon

The Jefferson Hill Tea Room

(2-4 p.m.) diners may enjoy the full dessert menu, tea sandwiches, quiche, soup, and favorite beverages. A basket of many kinds of Ashby and Connoisseur teas can be brought to your table. Or try a cup of delicious flavored coffee, latte' (a cross between hot chocolate and coffee), or cappuccino. The strawberry flavored lemonade is popular with children and summertime guests.

Naperville is a popular western Chicago suburb for businesses and shoppers. North Central College is located a few blocks from the Jefferson Hill Tea Room, as well as a great number of Victorian "painted lady" homes. Nearby Naper Settlement is Chicago-land's only living history museum. It depicts 19th century northern Illinois life and offers a full schedule of special events. I'm anxious to visit historic Centennial Beach and the DuPage River's River Walk that are popular Naperville attractions.

Jefferson Hill Tea Room was a pioneer tea room in the Midwest. It's one of the longest operating midwestern tea rooms I've found that isn't located in a hotel or department store. The menu was designed before the days in which foods such as quiche became household words in this part of the country. Kris related a story from the early days about a lady who was unfamiliar with the menu. She asked her server (with a straight face), "Now, what is this Swiss quickie?" My, we midwesterners **have** come a long way!

Naperville, Illinois

ASPARAGUS & HAM QUICHE

4 eggs
half & half (see amount in recipe directions)
1/2 teaspoon salt
dash pepper
dash nutmeg
4 ounces cooked ham, diced
1 cup canned asparagus, drained and patted dry
1 cup Swiss cheese, shredded
1-9 inch pie shell, partially baked

Preheat oven to 400°. Let a frozen pie shell stand for 10 minutes at room temperature, and bake for 7 minutes (do not prick shell). Remove from oven, and set aside. In a blender, place the eggs, and add half & half until the mixture reaches the 2 cup line. Add salt, pepper, and nutmeg. Blend until well mixed. Arrange the ham, asparagus, and cheese in the pie shell. Pour egg mixture over all, and bake 45 minutes at 325°-350°, until filling is firm, golden, and an inserted knife comes out clean.

BAKED CHICKEN SALAD

1 large chicken breast, cooked and diced
3-4 hard boiled eggs, diced
1 1/2 cups celery, chopped
1 can water chestnuts, drained
1/3 cup green onion, diced (optional)
1/2 cup mayonnaise
1-10 3/4 ounce cream of chicken soup
salt, to taste
pepper, to taste
1/2 teaspoon lemon juice (optional)
1/2 cup cheddar cheese, shredded
1/4-1/2 cup potato chips, crushed
1-9 inch pie shell, baked

Preheat oven to 350°. Mix all ingredients. Pour into baked pie shell. Top with grated cheese and chips. Bake for 20 minutes. Let set five minutes before serving. (Filling may be made the day ahead and refrigerated for later use.)

This a big favorite at Jefferson Hill. Some people come to have it for lunch each week.

LISA'S TEA TREASURES
WINNETKA, ILLINOIS

No matter how much I try to describe Lisa's Tea Treasures to my friends and acquaintances, it seems I don't do an adequate job. I'm not talking about amateur tea room travelers either. I'm talking about people more seasoned in tearoom-ese than me. They always comment that it is so much more than what they expected. I promise to try harder and will start by saying that proprietress, Susan Mangione, has definitely enhanced the concept of afternoon tea in the Midwest. It's an upscale tea room with touches of formality and elegance. The attentive service and soothing ambience complete the experience.

Two distinguishing features of Lisa's Tea Treasures are that it's a California-based tea room and a franchised operation. At this writing, there are 4 Lisa's in California. Winnetka, in the area known as Chicago's North Shore, is the only Lisa's in the Midwest. Susan says to expect to find more of them across the US soon. Her Winnetka version opened in November of 1994 in an area of town known as Hubbard Woods to local residents. Almost any map of Chicago will show Green Bay Road that runs parallel to Lake Michigan.

Founder, Lisa Strauss, is a former computer executive. In her travels to Singapore, she discovered British afternoon tea. She left her grueling job, and in 1992, opened the first Lisa's Tea Treasures in San Jose which showcases teas from England and around the world. It quickly outgrew its cottage and is now located in a Victorian mansion.

Susan Mangione was thinking about a new career when the Fortune 500 company she was working for decided to relocate to another city. When she read about the opportunity to franchise a tea room in a business magazine, she flew to California to do some sleuthing. She felt the Chicago area was ready for a Lisa's.

Plump tea cozies keep tea pots warm for hours at Lisa's. That's fortunate because I can't imagine going there and not tarrying for awhile. China biscuit barrels on each table are filled with oblaten wafers to be topped with lemon curd for an authentic English tea treat. You may select a hearty luncheon tea from one of eight on the "Afternoon Tea Times From Around the World" menu, or a lighter afternoon tea delight (also eight choices). A special version of tea is offered on a monthly basis "just in case there isn't enough to select from on the regular menu." "My Lady's Respite" is a particular favorite. It includes "a lovely Earl Grey Tea served with assorted tea sandwiches (chicken tarragon, smoked salmon, cucumber & mint, pesto, and corned beef), mini herb souffle, mini scones with Earl Grey double Devonshire cream, preserves, complemented by a mini cheese cake, a petit four, and a tea princess truffle." Each menu sounds equally tantalizing, and there's even a fat-free afternoon tea.

Your food will be presented by a server dressed in maid or butler's attire on a three-tiered muffin stand that rests on the floor by your table. Your tea will be served on Royal Doulton china decorated with delicate moss roses. The tea is of the loose leaf variety, and many choices are offered. Real tea drinkers often do not drink tea out of their homes because it is difficult to find tea served with as much attention to detail as the rest of the meal. This is not a problem at Lisa's. Crystal bells on the tables allow you to ring for service, or you can just settle back on your velvet Victorian sofa or armchair and feel satisfied.

After tea, the gift parlour affords a bit of shopping for gifts with tea themes or supplies for home tea service. The packaging on their house blends of tea is exquisite. You'll also want to explore the five rooms—all with different decorating themes and strains of classical music. There's a children's tea room and a men's library as well as three rooms with Victorian flavors.

At Lisa's, tea is professed to be one of "life's little pleasures." Quality teas and delicious tea treats are served in romantic surroundings—always fit for a "tea princess." Dust off that tiara, and head for Lisa's. (If you can't find yours, feel free to borrow mine.)

PINEHILL BED & BREAKFAST
OREGON, ILLINOIS

When you reserve time for a private, chocolate, tea party at Pinehill Bed and Breakfast in Oregon, Illinois, the mansion becomes your castle; and all that follows is your own, personal teadom.

Tea is a great equalizer. It's said that tea soothes the nerves or produces an energy burst—whatever your body is aching for. It's a drink for the soul and will provide whatever element is needed to keep you at your best. Chocolate is described as addictive, a wee bit sinful, and very soothing. At Pinehill B&B, tea and chocolate marry to provide a gladsome escape from the big, bad world.

The inn is an 1874 Italianate country villa with three rooms (all with private baths) plus a suite. Owned by Sharon Burdick, it has been honored with many awards including being chosen as one of the top inns of 1993 by *Country Inns* magazine. Pinehill is one of the stops along the Blackhawk Chocolate Trail, a collection of chocolate producers, shops, etc. in northwestern Illinois.

Chocolate became Pinehill's trademark almost accidently when Sharon needed to plan a theme for an open house in the 1990 Christmas season. She set up a display of impressive, decorated, fudge wreaths and added plenty of bows and pine branches for extra ambience. It was such a hit that it became the *Pinehill Fudge Collection* that delights fudge lovers year-round with over 30 kinds of exotic, signature fudge. New flavors are tested each season, and the favorites are added to the collection. The chocolate teas are an outgrowth of the *Fudge Collection* and the frenzy Sharon discovered people have about chocolate.

Tea parties are a private affair at Pinehill and may be scheduled as an afternoon or evening event any month of the year. Individuals or groups are welcome. Once Sharon books your party, the inn becomes your private domain.

The chocolate tea menu varies and depends on availability and discoveries of new chocolates. It is safe to say that you will not be disappointed with the edible display of fine American and imported chocolates. You'll delight in old favorites and make fast friends with new ones. Former guests alert Sharon of chocolate discoveries that they deem worthy of her chocolate teas.

Other treats include molds of the famous *Fudge Collection*. These are not cut into the traditional, limiting, one-inch squares. They're sitting there in three to eight pound mounds just daring you to shave away with reckless abandonment. The fudges are accompanied by an array of hot chocolates (of course), cappucinos, coffees, and teas. All drinks are of gourmet quality. Even the whipped cream flavors are unusual. A special, chocolate dessert may be prepared if your group is of sufficient size. For those of you who just can't loosen up or who are medically unable to consume caffeine or sweets, herbal teas and fresh fruits will give you something to do with your hands as you watch the chocoholics in your midst lose their inhibitions.

No description of a chocolate tea will adequately describe the experience because each person will relate to it differently. The ideas people have about chocolate are far-reaching. The psychological overtones are intense. I, for example, find that the freedom to eat as much chocolate as I want suddenly produces a satiated feeling and a poor appetite. I love chocolate but prefer it as a sensual experience—just letting it slowly melt and never allowing it to touch my teeth. Doug, on the other hand, prefers to shoot it in like popcorn kernels, chomping piece after piece—mashing it on his molars as if it's nothing special. (For having an attitude like that, he certainly seems to pack a lot of it in. I'll never forget the time I first saw him sacrilegiously munch the ears off a chocolate Easter bunny. I was horrified.)

And many of you know, afternoon tea is sort of the same way. Each person values a special part of it. A chocolate tea at Pine Hill provides all sorts of freedom for each partaker to enjoy the part of tea and chocolate she finds the most satisfying.

Oregon, Illinois

PINEHILL'S DARK CHOCOLATE CREAM FUDGE BASE

3 cups sugar
1/2 cup salted butter
1 1/2 cups evaporated milk
14 ounces mini marshmallows
4 cups semisweet chocolate mini-chips
2 teaspoons pure vanilla extract
3 cups filler*

Carefully heat and stir over medium burner the sugar, butter, milk, and marshmallows until mixture comes to a rolling boil. Continue to stir for an additional 5 minutes, being careful not to splash. Quickly add chips and vanilla extract, and stir until smooth. Add filler. Pour into buttered mold. Refrigerate overnight. Remove from mold and decorate. Makes 5 pounds of fudge.

PINEHILL'S BUTTERSCOTCH FUDGE BASE

3 cups sugar
1/2 cup salted butter
1 1/2 cups evaporated milk
14 ounces mini marshmallows
4 cups butterscotch chips
1 tablespoon pure orange extract
3 cups filler*

Follow directions for the dark chocolate fudge base, substituting the butterscotch chips and orange extract.

Use Sharon's base recipes to create the fudge of your dreams! Possibilities include ingredients such as pecans, Brazil nuts, raisins, cashews, Macadamia nuts, dried cranberries and other dried fruits, peanut butter chips, etc. Sharon would love to hear of any concoction that you find especially delicious.

RASPBERRY TEA ROOM
ELWIN, ILLINOIS

Jeanette Ball, co-owner of the Raspberry Tea Room, warned me when I called. She said the tea room she and Virginia Bilyeu own is probably the most busy tea room I'd ever see. I arrived at 2:00 on a Monday afternoon, and even at that hour, there was still a crowd.

This notable tea room is located in the Elwin Antique Mall, just off Interstate 72 at the Pana and Rt. 51 exit (or four miles south of Decatur on Rt. 51) which allows for easy motor access. I don't imagine to fact that Virginia offers 15 to 20 desserts daily hurts business either. Jeanette said they have many regular customers. "Sometimes they call and ask what we're having for lunch and I ask them, 'What should we have?'" That's how small town hospitality works.

Owners of the antique mall, located in an old motel building in the central Illinois town, asked Jeanette to operate the mall's dining facility after she'd advised them about the style of restaurant she felt was appropriate to accompany their business. At the time, she worked in her son's restaurant in nearby Moweaqua, was a former antique shop owner, and was still an antique show dealer. Her co-worker, Virginia, became excited about the idea and said they could operate as a team. Virginia was over 70 years old at the time.

The ladies named their venture the Raspberry Room because they had so many favorite recipes using raspberries. Jeanette cooks; and Virginia bakes...and bakes...and bakes. Even her pie crusts are made from scratch.

Customer favorites are the cashew chicken salad croissant, spinach salad, three salad plate, and the French onion soup. The raisin cheese grill, a sandwich with Swiss and American cheeses grilled on raisin bread with fresh apple slices, is a house specialty.

Elwin, Illinois

Quiches and other specials are offered daily. You can always count on one of Virginia's homemade muffins to accompany your meal.

The dessert list is a bonanza of tea room specialties. Try Milky Way, raspberry cream, Black Forest chocolate mousse, or pecan cream cheese pies. Or perhaps cake sounds more appealing. In that case, select the raspberry torte or chocolate raspberry cake. Or maybe a slice of turtle cheesecake would slide right down. I often think I could just skip eating and apply desserts like these straight to my hips—but why miss the fun?

"Gourmet Wednesday" is an evening event held in the cooler months of the year. A six course meal is served for well under $20 per person. Some customers come to every one. There's a choice of two entrees, and you may select your favorite dessert. Reservations are a must because they only cook for 50 guests. Jeanette says her husband often helps with these evening meals and says, "They are very relaxing, fun meals to serve."

Mismatched antique chairs and linens, old cupboards, and other antique accents help make the tea room cozy but unpretentious. It's a place that both men and women will feel comfortable. Jeanette is a primitive-style antique dealer and has a show space in the Elwin Antique Mall.

One of the highlights of the tea room's history came when actress, Ann Jillian, arrived in Decatur to perform for a cancer benefit production. She was treated to lunch at the Raspberry Room by her hosts. Jeanette said she was very gracious and spoke about the Raspberry Room when she was on stage.

The Raspberry Tea Room is highly recommended. Plan your trip so that you are flexible about the time you want to eat. Remember, you'll be jockeying for dining positions with many loyal, regular customers. You can browse through the huge antiques mall if there's a wait, and the meal will be worth the delay.

SAWDUST PIE

7 egg whites, unbeaten
1 1/2 cups white sugar
1 1/2 cups vanilla wafer crumbs
1 1/2 cups pecan pieces
1 1/2 cups shredded coconut
1-9 inch pie shell, unbaked

Preheat oven to 325°. Place all ingredients in a bowl, and blend with a spoon or spatula. Pour into unbaked pie shell, and bake until glossy and set (about 25-30 minutes). Do not over-bake.

Serve warm with sliced bananas and whipped cream. Serves 8

SWEET POTATO APPLE SALAD

2-16 ounce cans sweet potato pieces, drained
1-16 ounce can pineapple chunks, drained
4 red delicious apples, chopped (may leave on skins)
1/2 cup coconut, shredded
1/2 cup walnuts, chopped
12 ounce container whipped topping
3/4 cup mayonnaise

Place the first five ingredients in a large bowl. Gently fold in whipped topping and mayonnaise. Be careful not to break up the sweet potatoes. Sprinkle a few chopped walnuts on top for garnish.

Jeanette says this is very popular as an accompaniment to the many chicken dishes they serve.

Elwin, Illinois

AMISH SUGAR CREAM PIE

3/4 cup white sugar
1/8 teaspoon salt
2 1/2 cups half & half
1/4 cup brown sugar
1/4 cup cornstarch
1/2 cup margarine
1 teaspoon vanilla extract
1-9 inch pie shell, lightly baked
1/8 teaspoon cinnamon

Preheat oven to 475°. Lightly bake frozen pie shell according to package directions. If using a homemade crust, prick bottom and sides of crust thoroughly with fork. Bake for 8-10 minutes or until lightly browned. Cool. Lower oven temperature to 325°.

In medium saucepan, combine white sugar, salt, and half & half. Bring to a boil, stirring constantly. In second saucepan, combine brown sugar and cornstarch. Gradually stir in the hot half & half mixture using a wire whisk. Add margarine and cook mixture five minutes or until boiling and thickened, stirring constantly with the whisk. Simmer one minute. Stir in vanilla. Pour mixture into baked crust. Sprinkle with cinnamon. Bake 20 minutes or until top of pie is golden. Place on wire rack to cool. (Filling will be very "loose" but will thicken upon cooling.) Cool completely before serving.

Serves 10.

SEASONS OF LONG GROVE
LONG GROVE, ILLINOIS

It was precisely 2:30 on a summer afternoon in the historic village of Long Grove, Illinois. A bell chimed several times in the garden-like Seasons of Long Grove restaurant, and a voice announced over the speaker system, "Ladies and gentlemen, it is now half past two; and it's tea time." And tea time it was—in all its splendor.

Eight choices of black, green, and herbal loose teas with origins and descriptions were listed on the tea menu for customers' sipping enjoyment. A few of the unusual varieties were passion fruit peppermint, chamomile lemon, and cardamom cinnamon. My choice was the mango Ceylon, a fruit flavored tea. Our server recommended it, and I'll pass along the recommendation to you. A tea testing table in the restaurant's entrance invited guests to preview the scents and appearances of these fine teas.

Season's Mad Hatter tea savories were presented on a three-tiered plateau. The top plate included Jammin' Breads with imported Danish marmalade, uncooked strawberry jam, and whipped cream. The second plate was filled with Teanie Sandwiches, and a third showed off a selection of Neat Sweets. On the day we visited, the tea time menu was as follows:

Currant Scones
Lemon Chardonnay Biscuits
Strawberry Jam, Orange Marmalade, and Whipped Cream
Cucumber, Watercress, Boursin Cheese on White
Egg Salad and Edible Flowers on Wheat
Gravlox Salmon on Pumpernickel Crouton
Roast Beef and Crispy Onions on French Bread
Chocolate Pecan Triangles
Fresh Fruit Tarts
Chocolate Dipped Strawberries

Long Grove, Illinois

It was an elaborate spread that surpassed my tea time expectations. Compared to many tea menus, Season's was less rich and sweet—for which I was thankful. Champagne may be substituted for tea at an additional charge for an extra special celebration.

Doug couldn't resist sampling from the luncheon buffet, the restaurant's largest draw. It is a unique gourmet parade of several entrees, hot vegetables, breads, cheeses, and approximately eight salad selections. There are may be coleslaw, pasta, and potato salads; but they will be disguised in dressings and garnishments that will make your meal memorable. Each item on the luncheon bar is clearly labeled. Doug was well-pleased with his meal. He said that it wasn't all "chick chow" (his summation of tea room food), and that there were many items men would enjoy. The menu rotates about every three days. Entrees on the day we visited were London broil pepper steak in a Zinfandel sauce and rotini pasta with chicken in fresh basil oil. A reoccurring favorite is the basil mashed potatoes. Grilled salmon in lemon caper vinaigrette, jicama and cabbage slaw, and penne pasta with fresh vegetables in pesto were three of the day's salads. In addition, an ala carte menu, sandwiches, and soups are available, as well as selections from the pastry chef. Crème brûlé and key lime pie are two of my recommendations. Many of the foods from executive chef, J.C. Villegas' kitchen are seasoned liberally with fresh herbs and decorated with edible flowers.

Season's is a large restaurant seating 200 guests; but tea time is kept cozy by grouping tea guests in the section that wraps around the sun-drenched, brick-floored, atrium area in the front part of the dining room.

The Mangel Company is the owner of the Seasons of Long Grove restaurant. John and Heidi Mangel and their two sons, John and David, own several businesses within the village. Heidi is the creator of the blooming, country garden effect in Seasons. The decor will be changed to reflect each season of the year. A garden patio area is complete with a wood-burning grill and spit with rotisserie.

The town of Long Grove is a pastoral village just northwest of Chicago. A covered bridge welcomes visitors to its quaint downtown business district with many turn-of-the-century specialty stores. The town has been renovated in a way that retains its old-fashioned, country atmosphere.

Although tea at Seasons is all that is proper, it also has a side that is just plain fun. According to general manager of Seasons, John Wise, hats are the crowning glory of the Mad Hatter's afternoon tea. Each afternoon, the emblazoned, flamboyant hats are displayed in the lobby; and guests are invited to make their tea time costume selections. They like to take their time when choosing the hat to reflect their moods and temperaments. A large mirror is an aid for discovering just the right match. Men are not off the (hat) hook. A collection of fine derbies and other theme hats give them a chance to play along and to share the fun the women have. There are even hats for babies. "Our hat inventory is up to about 85 now because we just had a wedding tea here last week," said John. The splendorous hats, lavished with flowers, netting, silk, and ribbons, are made by Mangles of Long Grove. The next step may be to sell them because some tea guests can't bear to part with their hats at the afternoon's end.

Tea time at Seasons of Long Grove is worthy of a grand hotel, but it's much less expensive and in a less formidable setting. I like to think it's a preview of how tea will be in heaven—but I'm sure I'll have a much more angelic tea time partner there.

Long Grove, Illinois

GRAVLOX SALMON SANDWICHES

1/2 pound fresh salmon fillet
1 ounce Scotch whiskey or tequila
1 teaspoon fresh, cracked black pepper
3 tablespoons salt
1 1/2 tablespoons sugar
1 teaspoon fresh dill weed
5 slices pumpernickel bread
1/2 cup mayonnaise
1/2 teaspoon Dijon mustard
2 tablespoons butter

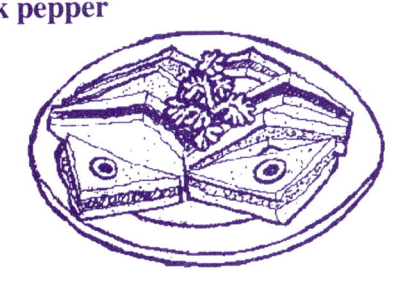

Pull the bones out of the fresh salmon with a needle-nosed pliers. Place fish, with skin side down, in a glass or metal pan at least 2 inches deep. Pour liquor over the fish. Sprinkle fish with the pepper. Mix salt and sugar in a cup, and sprinkle over the top of the fish to coat. Sprinkle dill over the fish. Take a spoon, collect any liquor from the pan, and pour over the fish. Place a glass or metal bowl or pan directly on top if the fish. Add at least 2 pounds of rice, etc. to the bowl to act as a weight. Place fish, weighted with the rice, in the refrigerator—do not cover—for three days. Air and the weight of the bowl will force sugar and salt into the fish—drying and curing it.

After three days, remove the weight from the fish. Place fish on cutting board, and with a sharp carving knife, slowly slice lengthwise into paper thin strips. Remove the over-seasoned top layer and discard. Continue slicing until down to the bottom skin.

With a cookie cutter, cut out desired shapes in the bread. Toast bread lightly. Mix mayonnaise and mustard in a cup. Put a light dollop of this on each piece. Cut salmon into 1-1/2 inch pieces. Fold and place on the bread. Top each with a fresh dill sprig to serve. Makes about 12 sandwiches.

John says this is one of the best tea sandwiches they offer. It is an economical method for curing your own fresh salmon.

THE SPICERY TEA ROOM
TUSCOLA, ILLINOIS

When talk turns to tea rooms in central Illinois, the Spicery Tea Room in Tuscola, is usually mentioned first. The Spicery has earned a reputation as the "grande dame" of tea rooms in that part of the state.

Although the tea room's fame has been earned by owner, Donna Kidwell, and her staff, it got a jump-start by an accidental phone call. Donna said she was ready to change her phone number because she kept receiving insurance related calls. One of the wrong numbers was a reporter from a local newspaper who was calling about an insurance adjustment. When Donna explained she was talking to a tea room operator—not an insurance agent, the reporter decided a tea room sounded interesting and asked for an interview. Business boomed after the article was printed, and the phone number was never changed.

Donna opened Wood, Tin and Lace and Stencils gift shop four years before she opened the tea room. Out-of-town customers often asked if there was a tea room in Tuscola. Having a tea room had been her dream, and the inquiries prompted her to open the Spicery Tea Room directly across the street from her store. In 1993, she opened a third venture, Pineapple Primitives—another gift shop, next door to Wood, Tin and Lace.

The main floor of a 1909 Sears and Roebuck residence houses the Spicery in small town Tuscola (population 4327). Burgundy paint brightens the old woodwork, and the floors are gleaming oak. Lace curtains cover the windows; and a painted, floral, stencil pattern provides wall decoration. Mismatched vintage items: tables, chairs, cupboards, linens, and framed Victorian prints complete the old-fashioned atmosphere.

A meal at the Spicery is a retreat to days before the invention of fast foods. The food quality is a major contributor to the tea room's fame. The menu is an array of tea room classics: soups, salads, quiches, casseroles, and desserts. Everything is prepared using old-time "from scratch" methods. The Spicery also specializes in homemade crackers, poppyseed salad dressing, breads, and muffins. Although many items seem sinfully rich, all the menu selections are naturally low in calories and fats; and the menu has been improved by the American Heart Association. Donna's consideration for health lingers from the days she was a registered nurse.

Special menu items are offered daily. "The chicken pecan quiche started as a special, but people want it all the time. They're disappointed if we don't have it," said Donna. I loved the chicken pecan quiche with its nutty, crumbly crust and blend of chicken, pecan, and cheese flavors; but I'll admit I've admired everything I've sampled at the Spicery. The homemade crackers are paper-thin, wheat wafers with a texture and taste that must drive other crackers to their boxes whimpering in shame. Other treats are chilled strawberry soup, lemon asparagus soup, and turkey bake casserole. The white chocolate cheese cake is testimony to the Spicery's dedication to taking care of central Illinois dessert lovers. It's made with a low fat cocoa but is smooth, rich, and creamy; and it's topped with a puree of raspberries and brandy.

Tea selections at the Spicery include hot tea, iced tea accented with lemon slices and fresh mint from the herb garden, house tea, and Texas tea. The chilled house and Texas teas are sweetened and flavored with fruit juices.

Much of the Spicery's recipe repertoire is owed to Donna's mother, Doris McKenna, who lives in Arizona. When Donna was a child, her father was a flyer in the U.S. Armed Forces. Donna and her mother stayed with her grandmother in New York State. They liked to travel to tea rooms in their area, and her mother would prepare special meals when her father returned home on leave. "My recipes are my mother's. I use them and modify them," said Donna.

Tuscola, Illinois

There are many nearby attractions to see when you visit the Spicery Tea Room. The sister gift shops are exemplary, or you could visit the Factory Stores outlet mall—also in Tuscola. Amish country, Rockome Gardens, or the area's fine festivals such as the Arcola Broom Corn Festival and the Arcola Raggedy Ann and Andy Festival provide family entertainment. The University of Illinois at Champaign is a half hour drive from Tuscola.

I extend an urgent recommendation to readers to visit the Spicery Tea Room. It's an experience no fancier of tea room cuisine should dare miss.

TURKEY and ASPARAGUS BAKE

1 pound fresh or 10 ounces frozen asparagus
1 pound ground turkey
1 cup chopped onion
1/2 cup chopped red pepper
6 eggs
1 cup flour
2 cups milk
1/4 cup Parmesan cheese
1 teaspoon lemon pepper
3/4 teaspoon salt
3/4 teaspoon tarragon
1 cup shredded Swiss cheese

Cut asparagus into 1 1/2 inch pieces, and cook until tender. Drain and set aside. In a skillet, saute turkey, onion, and red pepper until vegetables are tender and turkey is no longer pink. Remove from heat and drain. Spray a 9" x 13" x 2" pan with vegetable spray. Place meat mixture in the pan, and top with asparagus.

In a medium bowl, combine eggs, milk, flour, Parmesan cheese, lemon pepper, salt, and tarragon. Beat with a mixer until smooth. Pour egg mixture over the meat and asparagus. Bake in a preheated 425° oven for 20 minutes or until eggs are thickened. Sprinkle with Swiss cheese, and bake 3-5 minutes longer for cheese to melt. Serve immediately.

Recipe serves 10. Each serving may be garnished with cooked asparagus spears, lemon slices, or red pepper rings.

Donna says that there are only 263 calories per serving in this dish. It's a good family meal because it is excellent frozen and reheated.

THE TEA PARTY CAFE
GENEVA, ILLINOIS

I tell you—these tea room owners are a hardy bunch! They seem to be able to beat all odds. Lucinda Williams, owner of the Tea Party Cafe in the Old Mill Market, opened her tea room in December of 1992—sort of. Within days of the Tea Party's opening, Geneva's State Street bridge closed; and traffic was routed away from the tea room. The street remained closed for nine months. At times, the tea room's parking lot was a resting place for construction equipment instead of customers' vehicles. Luckily for Williams, construction workers are known to have big appetites. The turning point arrived when State Street reopened; and Divine Desserts, a popular, gourmet bakery, became a tenant of the Old Mill Market.

Lucinda's original intent was to serve only coffees, teas, and muffins. That idea didn't last long. Soon customers started to request soups. Lucinda added soup to the Tea Party menu. When they requested lunches, she complied. Finally, the tea room opened for breakfast and dinner, as well.

Lucinda's successful philosophy has been to offer a limited menu of items that she does best and are not available in other local restaurants. She said, "People will come to you if you have something special. They want things you can't find down the street." The Tea Party Cafe is a bread lover's paradise, and is known for its heavenly desserts (supplied by Divine Desserts, of course), "muffin meals," and its fabled chicken salad.

Breakfast to dinner, you can be assured it will taste homecooked. Lucinda hand-selects produce and meats from a neighborhood market to monitor the quality of her ingredients. Sandwiches are served on crusty, homemade rolls. Dill and vegetable breads are the most popular with cheese, four-grain, and sourdough following closely behind. Seventy pounds or more of gourmet chicken salad is sold each week. The customer favorite is punctuated with crisp pea pods and water chestnuts and bathed in a creamy, mayonnaise base. What a treat!

I was impressed by the homemade salad selections. A diet sampler plate includes: carrot, cucumber, coleslaw, and pasta salads. The salads are low in calories (only 300) and in fat (2 grams). Another sampler plate includes the famous Tea Party chicken salad.

Ten kinds of muffin meals include pasta salad and chips. Special English muffins, in a variety of flavors, are paired with interesting fillings. Two examples would be the apple strudel muffin topped with apples and melted cheddar cheese or sliced chicken on a honey oat raisin bran English muffin topped with mozzarella and pineapple. Of course, the chicken salad is available as a muffin meal—this time on a sourdough muffin.

The extensive dessert menu might include flourless rum chocolate cake, strawberry cream torte, turtle brownies, numerous cheesecakes, filled eclairs, carrot cake, thick cherry bars...need I say more?

Afternoon tea service is available by reservation. Lucinda needs lead time to be certain she has the proper breads and desserts on hand. Customers may have their choices of 16 teas. Tea sandwiches, fruits, and miniature sweets complete the tea menu. Tea desserts at the Tea Party Cafe are special petit fours such as carrot cake, strawberry custard torte with whipped cream, French vanilla cheesecake, or a nut cup with mousseline sauce.

The Tea Party Cafe has comfortable, eclectic decor. It reminds me of pictures I've seen of quaint, European tea rooms. The wooden bakery cases showcase bakery delights from Divine Desserts, handsome muffins, scones, and loaves of bread. Antiques are displayed on the walls. China is a relaxed mixture of black and

Geneva, Illinois

white with a Art Nouveau look and old-fashioned floral patterns. There's no cookie cutter look here. Everywhere you look, there's something interesting to examine.

Geneva makes an excellent vacation spot. The Metra train will take you straight to the heart of downtown Chicago within an hour. Or there's plenty to see and do in Geneva. There is a wealth of historic buildings and Victorian homes to view and over 100 shops and restaurants. St. Charles, Batavia, and Aurora are nearby with a multitude of shops and malls. Geneva is in Kane County, home to the notable Kane County antique and flea markets. The Herrington, built in 1835 as a trading post and remodeled into a creamery in 1874, now is an inn with fine accommodations. It's across the street from the Tea Party Cafe and located at the edge of the Fox River. The Oscar Swan Bed and Breakfast (8 rooms) would be another interesting place to stay during your tour of Geneva. Geneva is located along the scenic Fox River Valley with many miles of the Illinois Prairie Path Trails for hiking and biking. Bicycles are available to rent at reasonable prices by the hour or day.

Geneva is host to four festivals each year: April's Historic Geneva Fest, June's Annual Swedish Days, September's Festival of the Vine, and December's Geneva Christmas Walk. Complete schedules are available by calling 708-232-6060.

Even though Lucinda's got an excellent thing going at the Tea Party Cafe, her entrepreneuring spirit drives her tirelessly to improve and perfect her product. She recently revamped the tea room's floor plan to better meet her customers' needs by supplying a larger variety through an authentic Italian deli. However, she managed to keep the charm of the Tea Party Cafe intact. Thank you, Lucinda!

FRUKTSOPPA
(SWEDISH FRUIT SOUP)

1 cup dried prunes
2 quarts cold water
1/2 cup raisins
1/4 cup sago*
1/2 cup currants
1 small cinnamon stick
1/2 cup dried apples
1/2 cup dark corn syrup

Place the prunes, raisins, currants and apples in the water. Cover, and soak overnight. In the morning, add sago and cinnamon stick. Simmer, covered, over very low heat 1 1/2 hours. Add the corn syrup, and continue to simmer slowly for 1 hour. Chill the soup, and serve it cold.

Serves 9-12 guests.

*Sago is a dark cherry sauce which may be purchased at a gourmet food store. It is a Swedish product. Cherry juice and liqueur may be substituted for the sago.

Lucinda says this is a very popular take-out item and she sells it by the pint. (An advance order may be necessary.) Geneva's annual Swedish Days festival is held in June.

TIARA MANOR BED AND BREAKFAST AND TEA ROOM
PARIS, ILLINOIS

The Tiara Manor Tea Room is a case of Victorian elegance at its finest. From the eighteen foot gazebo in the formal garden, to the richly appointed tea room and gift shop of fine collectibles, to the four bed and breakfast rooms on the Gothic mansion's second floor—you'll find yourself enveloped in time-honored luxury.

Jo Marie Nowarita said, with a hint of a retained Chicago accent, that her grandparents had lived in the small central Illinois town of Paris; and she'd always felt a fondness for the community. Afternoons in Paris meant afternoon tea with Grandma. "It was our special time," explained Jo Marie. "You used your pretty things and dishes. And the men weren't home from work yet. We always made time for a cup of tea and a snack." As her husband, Richard, and she grew older, they found they shared a love for antiques. They first restored their home, an 1873 Italianate. In March of 1992, they opened the bed and breakfast rooms in the Gothic house formerly owned by D.D. Houston, a Paris judge and land owner; and the tea room opened in July of the same year. Tiara Manor was furnished with museum quality antiques acquired during its restoration period.

The tea room, like the rest of the house, has been restored to antebellum Civil War grandeur by Jo Marie with patterned carpeting, wallpaper with lush rose bouquets, and richly upholstered dining chairs. Crystal chandeliers, two of the house's seven fireplaces, old photographs, and a collection of French style prints of ladies compound the Victorian aura.

Victorians upheld family relationships as a foremost priority, as does Jo Marie. Most of the staff is comprised of family members who cook and serve delicacies in ample portions. Starr, the Nowarita's oldest daughter, trained at the Indianapolis Culinary Institute and is the tea room's chef. Vinnie and Amy Jo help with serving and other tasks. Jo Marie supervises the tea room and fine gift store, while Richard is more involved with the bed and breakfast business.

My chicken pecan quiche had a top layer of nuts that were sweetened by a careful oven toasting. It was accompanied by a tossed salad and a thick slice of very fresh, homemade, herbed bread. Several entree salads and sandwiches on homemade breads were also noted on the menu blackboard at the tea room's entrance. Jo Marie explained she'd increased the number of sandwich selections to gratify the appetites of the numerous male customers. More and more men are discovering Tiara Manor's homemade cuisine and elegant atmosphere make it a perfect place for business luncheons.

Although portions are generous, few diners are able to resist the tray of desserts that is presented tableside. Their minds are easy to read—"I'll diet tomorrow!"

Valentine Chocolate Lovers and Dickens Christmas teas are regular Tiara Manor events complete with special music. These teas are small portions of sweets and savories served in numerous courses. Because many tea takers are experiencing their first tea parties of this sort, there is a short presentation at the beginning of the events explaining some of the customs and history of the formal tea. Jo Marie enjoys these soirees immensely and says they have always been sold out—she's never needed to advertise.

Although the old home and tea room are picture-postcards of charm and elegance, and the food is exemplary, I found the tea room's greatest treasure to be Jo Marie's endearing Victorian spirit of hospitality and grace. She sees the tea room as her chance to entertain company everyday. When you visit Tiara Manor, make a point of introducing yourself and telling her how you found your way to her little piece of heaven.

WINDOWPANES TEA ROOM
OAKLAND, ILLINOIS

Many times we're afraid to leave behind lifestyles that pay those annoying bills and follow our dreams. I'll plead guilty to that charge. It took two years of deliberation for Linda and Gary Miller to leave their old lives behind (she was a bookkeeper and he an assistant manager for a hotel chain), but in the summer of 1992 they joined the growing ranks of midwestern entrepreneurs. "I felt a part of this place the first time we looked at it," said Linda.

Built in 1878 by S.M. Cash, the Inn-on-the-Square is a landmark in a village where welcoming signs proclaim the town to be "An Illinois Certified City—Population 1000." The inn rests on the north side of the town square which is complete with a statue of a Civil War soldier. It's large, square, and white. Eight pillars grace the front, and there are dozens of windows with many panes of glass. (I counted 24 panes in one window.) It looks like a building that would be found in New England, rather than America's heartland.

The interior of the building is equally impressive. The room to the left of the foyer is a front parlor with painted, wood paneled walls and a fireplace. It is used as a private dining or meeting room. To the right of the foyer, is the Windowpanes Tea Room. Immediately, my eyes were drawn to the huge, colonial style fireplace at the end of the room. It's the type of fireplace I've seen in the kitchens of early American museum homes—the kind in which hearthside cooking is done. The hand-hewn ceiling beams were harvested from a Civil War vintage barn. Ruby glass door panels, etched with white flowers, were hung horizontally to make area dividers in the tea room. Originally, the panels were part of the west entrance doors to the house. The walls of the tea room were lined with windows of many panes (Spring cleaning must be an invigorating experience). Each window was accented with a candlestick light.

Windowpanes Tea Room

An open staircase in the foyer leads visitors heavenward to the three beautiful guest rooms—each with private bath and a library for socializing, reading, or television watching. Also located on the second floor, is a dress shop and a shop with fine gifts. In the basement is an antique store full of well-arranged antiques, and the back of the foyer holds Granny's Nook with handmade gifts.

The S.M. Cash family occupied the mansion from 1878-1958. Great-nephew, Dr. Rolla Foley, purchased the home in 1958. He'd been a Quaker missionary in Israel and Lebanon from 1938-1944. Foley wanted the home for his retirement residence and a museum for his many artifacts and antiques. The basement would be a dormitory for Palestinian music students studying at nearby universities. Dr. Foley died in 1970, and his dreams were never realized. He succeeded in stripping the home of its Victorian qualities and replacing them with a Colonial flavor. (Victorian popularity was not as prevalent in the 1960's.)

After it had been abandoned for nine years, Max and Carolyn Coons, Oakland area farmers, took pity on the grand mansion. In 1986 they finished Dr. Foley's restoration plans, added the bed and breakfast rooms, and the tea room. The tea room was so popular that Linda says she was careful to keep things "status quo" when the Millers moved in.

The Windowpanes Tea Room's decor appeals to men, but women love it too. The fireplace and beams impart a substantial atmosphere. Linda has a knack of mixing Victorian accents with the colonial to soften the primitive look and to create visual contrast. An example of this is the Victorian parlor set that rests in front of the rustic stone fireplace.

The menu is a variety of sandwiches, a quiche and soup du jour, and salads. A daily special such as chicken fettucini is always available. The French onion soup is a Windowpanes favorite. It's topped with bread and mozzarella cheese and is broiled to perfection. It was very hot, slightly sweet, and extremely

Oakland, Illinois

flavorful—some of the best I've sampled. I enjoyed the seafood quiche and admired the moist blueberry bread with its plump berries; but my meal's highlight was the lettuce salad topped with roasted sunflower seeds and accompanied by Windowpanes's sweet, poppyseed dressing. Linda reported there's usually not a drop left in the souffle cups, and that's why they recently started to bottle the dressing for retail and wholesale markets.

The white chocolate mousse pie is the dessert favorite, but I was well satisfied with a weighty wedge of cheesecake topped with red raspberries. It was dusted lightly with nutmeg. Another popular dessert selection is the croissundae that comes in two sizes with ice cream that may be topped with caramel or hot fudge sauce. Both are expertly concocted in the Windowpane's kitchen.

If you like sweetened tea, be sure to try the robust, house, orange-spice version.

Linda is the tea room baker, chef, and hostess. Gary is the evening chef on Fridays and Saturdays from 5-8 p.m. He also serves a meal from 11 a.m.-2 p.m. on Sundays. Herb-roasted prime rib is the house specialty.

"Although Oakland is not close to any major towns, it's often a central location," said Linda."It's a good place for business meetings and seminars." Oakland is in the center of the Decatur, Champaign, Charleston, Terra Haute circuit; and is only 15 miles east of the Amish settlements in Arthur and Arcola. Other nearby attractions include the University of Illinois, Eastern Illinois University, or the Lincoln Log Cabin State Park (a fascinating place). Oakland is the perfect place to relax. You can sit under the trees in the town square park, visit the old-fashioned soda fountain or antique shops. Golfing and swimming facilities are close at hand. The Rutherford home is a museum in Oakland, filled with artifacts from the family who lived there. Dr. Rutherford left the comforts of the East to fulfill his dream of caring for frontier people. The Museum of Christian Heritage honors the disappearing country churches that used to dot the midwestern prairies (call for hours).

Oakland is host to a June quilt show and the popular mid-September Corn and Bean Festival.

Linda said giving customers pleasure is a very enjoyable part of her work. They smile and are apt to stay for a long time as they relax and enjoy the tea room. I asked Linda about how she viewed the change in her lifestyle. She reported she and Gary are enjoying working from their home and for themselves; and because their past jobs were very intense, they don't notice increased work loads. She said it's nice to not always have concern for upkeep of two work vehicles, and she can even shop for clothes without leaving her home in the upstairs boutique.

They say dreams are what our country is made from. Oakland and Inn-on-the-Square residents have had their shares of dreaming. Dr. Rutherford made it to the West to care for the frontiersmen. Dr. Foley started to work on his dream a little too late, but the Coons' dream was to restore the splendor of the old mansion; and they did it in fine style. Then the Millers continued the tradition by reaching for the American dream of self-employment. Plan a little weekend get-away to Oakland to reflect on your life, have lunch in the Windowpanes Tea Room, relax in one of the homey guest rooms at Inn-on-the Square; and as you tuck yourself in after a day of introspection, don't forget to have "sweet dreams." They're on the house!

Oakland, Illinois

CRAB & COUNTRY HAM OVER PASTA

1 pound fresh pasta
2 tablespoons butter
2 tablespoons flour
3/4 cup milk
3/4 cup half & half
3 tablespoons parmesan cheese
2 tablespoons dry sherry (optional)
1/8 teaspoon cayenne pepper, or to taste
salt, to taste
pepper, to taste
1 tablespoon vegetable oil
1 bunch green onions, chopped
1 red pepper, cut in julienne strips
8 ounces cooked crab meat (may use imitation)
4 ounces country ham, cut in julienne strips

Cook pasta. Set aside and keep warm. Melt butter in a medium saucepan. Add flour and blend to form a roux. Whisk in milk and half & half. Add cheese, sherry, cayenne pepper, salt, and pepper. Set aside. Heat oil in skillet. Saute onions and red pepper. Add to milk mixture. Add crab and ham. Serve over hot, drained pasta.

Serves 4 dinner or 8 luncheon guests.

INDIANA

Indiana

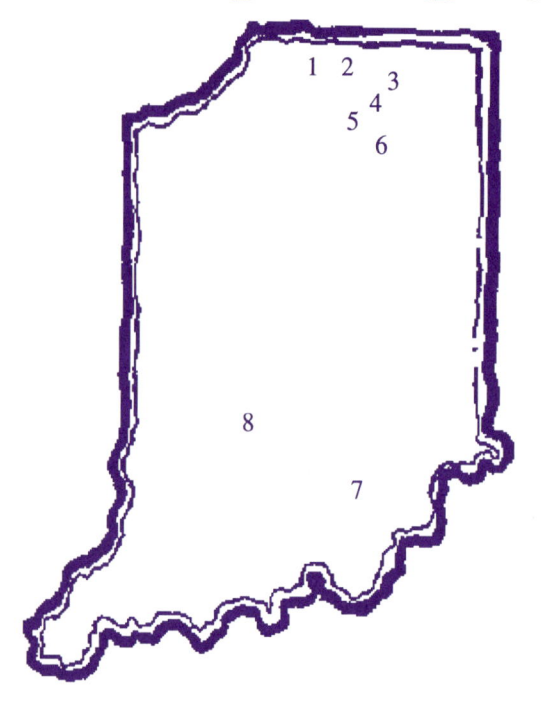

1. The Queen Anne Inn, South Bend
2. Rose Arbor Tea Room, Mishawaka
3. Trolley Cafe, Goshen
4. The Tea Room, Elkhart
5. The Victorian Guest House, Nappanee
6. The Good Stuff, Warsaw
7. The Story Inn, Story
8. Almost Home Tea Room, Greencastle

ALMOST HOME TEA ROOM
GREENCASTLE, INDIANA

"All our friends said we should have a tea room, but they never gave us any money!" said Gail Smith with a laugh. The efforts the of Almost Home owner and her partner, Sara Bridges, are well-known in their rural Indiana town where they became famous for their yearly Christmas craft show that drew 1600 people in its last year. A county sheriff was needed to direct traffic at Sara's country home, and truckers were radioing warnings of a ruckus up the road. "We're ambitious, but we're not rich," said Gail. She'd been bitten by the tea room bug when vacationing in Kentucky, and Almost Home became the first of several tea rooms in their part of the state.

I asked the ladies what they thought was the unique element of their tea room. They referred the question to a waitress who was quick to answer. "The food is wonderful. A lot of people say they go to a lot of tea rooms, but our food is the best." Gail mused, "I wonder if they're lying." The waitress shot that idea down immediately. "No! The people that say that have been to a lot of places. I wish you'd go down to Florida and teach them how to make chicken salad. We have a dressing that is so good!"

Sara said that the broccoli soup is the thing that brings people to Almost Home. "One lady comes in and says, 'I have to have my fix today.' Today one lady had seconds, and another came in for six bowls to go!" She said they have a long list of popular soups. Spinach garden, peanut butter, creamy green bean, carrot, and macaroni with cheese are just a few.

Gail described their food as homemade and delicious. "Everything's homemade, from scratch, except croissants and potato chips," she said. "And some people think we make our own potato chips, but we don't. It's the brand we use that makes them special."

Their tuna salad is made with egg noodles for a different

twist of a common recipe and came from Gail's grandmother's files. Wednesday is the ever-popular broccoli casserole day. The ladies agree that their best seller is the Almost Home Favorite with a small salad, small soup, and a half sandwich. Two of their salad dressings are homemade: blue cheese and the sweet and sour raspberry vinaigrette.

At least four or five desserts that should carry government health warning labels tempt visitors each day. On the day my husband and I visited, they had cherry cordial cream pie, French silk pie, chocolate Linzer tart with raspberry topping and ground almonds, strawberry pizza, and Mississippi mud pie made with their own homemade ice cream. They asked Doug how he liked his mud pie. He replied, "If the catfish knew how good this was, they'd jump the banks and be sitting out at your front door." They liked that answer and said it's a favorite—even in twenty degree below zero weather.

If you're having an extremely blessed day, you'll arrive on a day that Gail's baked her grand champion apple pie. Sara says Gail's the only one allowed to make the pie, but Gail said, "I do solicit help when it comes to cutting up the apples."

The tea room is decorated in a pure country style and is overflowing with grace and charm. They said, "We wanted it pretty but not too feminine. When men come in, they think they won't get full; but if they come in one time—they're sold, and they'll be back."

This year, Almost Home was honored by the state's lieutenant governor. He picked the tea room as one of the "Hidden Treasures of Indiana." The state published a map of one-tank vacation trips. Almost Home is listed under the Cataract Falls region which is a natural treasure with an exceptional waterfall, lake, and fishing areas. Other points of interest in Cataract Falls are the Cataract General Store, the Billie Creek Village General Store, The Seminary Place Bed & Breakfast, and the Suit's Us Bed & Breakfast. Tour busses sometimes plan stops at Almost Home

Greencastle, Indiana

because they have seating for 46.

Greencastle has a very active development center that is well-known for attracting industry. Walmart, Fashion Bug, and Sherwin Williams all have large centers in town. De Pauw University is there too. The town has managed to retain its quiet atmosphere in spite of all the expansion. "It's a neat place to be," said Gail.

Their menu introduction reads, "Welcome, our home is open to God, sunshine, and friends." But I think that means us too. I hope you get a chance to visit Gail and Sara at Almost Home for a gooey slice of dessert or a sizable helping of their southern Hoosier hospitality.

CREAM OF BROCCOLI SOUP

1/4 cup cooking oil or butter
1/2 medium onion, chopped
1 carrot, shredded
1 rib celery, chopped
1 pound broccoli (1 medium head),
    chopped florets and peeled stems
1/2 cup flour
3 to 4 cups chicken broth
2 cups milk
2 cups half & half

1/2 pound American processed cheese food, cubed
2 teaspoons lemon juice
1 teaspoon white pepper
2 teaspoons Worcestershire sauce
1 teaspoon salt, or to taste

Saute broccoli florets in oil until softened but still bright green. Remove from oil and reserve. Add onion, carrot, and celery to oil, and saute until soft. Stir flour into the oil and vegetable mixture until it is mixed in. Add chicken broth, milk, and half & half to the sauteed mixture, and cook until slightly thickened. Add reserved broccoli florets, cheese, lemon juice, pepper, Worcestershire sauce, and salt. Heat on low to medium heat, until hot.

Gail and Sara offer this recipe as a close facsimile for their broccoli soup recipe. They use a commercial ingredient or two not available to the general public.

THE GOOD STUFF
WARSAW, INDIANA

Mallory Miniear is a kind of tempest in a tea room—she's continually simmering with good ideas for her petite, French-inspired cafe with European artifacts aplenty. It's a showcase of her creativity, and she likes to say, "If you can imagine it—we can create it!"

A third-generation floral designer with 21 years of experience, she's found she doesn't miss that business. She says, "Food has filled that void." As a floral designer, she had the opportunity to be involved in special events that contracted caterers. She knew she could do better than some of what she saw. When the building just one door down from the floral shop emptied, Mallory decided it would be perfect for her custom-styled catering service. Soon, she found her customers asking for a way to purchase her products on a more regular basis. She decided to open an "unusual and quaint" tea room such as those she loves to visit when she travels, and she did just that in October of 1992.

Mallory quickly found out that both businesses needed her full-time attention. When an employee offered to buy the floral business, she knew she should sell it so that she could devote attention to her new baby—the tea room.

Wire ice cream chairs snuggle up to tables with teal, rose, and peach floral tablecloths. Hand-painted trompe l'oeil murals and French graffiti such as Au Revoir near the door and Merci Beaucoup decorate the walls. A water dispenser with mineral water that the French so dearly love is against one wall so that customers may help themselves. Franciscan dinnerware with old-fashioned apple blossoms are palettes for the artistic creations that are served on them.

The menu is listed on a huge blackboard. "We have no french fries. Everything is fresh, hand-chopped, baked, steamed, or boiled," said Mallory. The two items that vie as reigning champions on the Good Stuff's menu are the Swiss dill turkey salad on a croissant and the cashew chicken salad croissant. Trying to decide between the two is sort of like deciding whether you want to be a multi-millionaire or have a perfect body. Both alternatives sound like they have possibilities. Mallory is partial to the Swiss dill turkey salad, and I can't say that I blame her. A hint of dill marries the other dressing ingredients to make a creamy, soul-satisfying, sandwich filling. She pre-warned me that it was addictive, and in about seven days I'd get the urge for it when I was far away. I must admit, I've thought about dredging through my recipe file for my dill dip recipe from Cedar Rapids, Iowa, (the dill dip capital of the Midwest) to see what I could come up with; but I know the atmosphere and the company at the Good Stuff are flavor enhancers I couldn't replicate. That's enough drooling about turkey salad.

Two other spiffy entrees are the mini croissant lunch and the turkey provolone hero, and mushroom bisque and cold asparagus were the soups du jour. The tea room also serves other intriguing sounding varieties of "potage" such as curried tomato bisque, Swiss potato, cream of Reuben, cold cucumber, and cottage celery. What can I say but ooo-la-la!

Desserts such as cranberry almond muffins (recipe to follow), a variety of gourmet cookies, triple chocolate cheesecake, and white chocolate mousse will satisfy the sweet tooth without a hitch.

Imported cheeses such as English Darby sage and Cotswold or aged white Canadian cheddar are served and the crisp, wrapped bread sticks are a special treat.

Coffee beans are for sale at the Good Stuff for home brewing. Mallory says the favorites are the white heather, butterscotch rum, and hazelnut. Good quality teas, mineral waters, and rootbeer or cream soda in old-fashioned bottles are also available.

Warsaw is located in Kosciusko County (named after

Warsaw, Indiana

Thaddeus Kosciusko, a young Polish noble-man who fought in the American revolution) with 99 lakes. The normal population is around 25,000 people, but in the summer it swells to nearly 100,000, and is just south of Indiana's Amish country. Indiana's "Beaches and Backroads" publication says Warsaw is located in Indiana's antique country. Warsaw's Biblical Gardens is an oasis rich in beauty near the shores of Center Lake in downtown Warsaw. It features over 80 plants mentioned in the Bible.

Even though the tea room seems to be well-established and has no visible rough edges, its owner says, "I feel like we're in infancy and growing." And the adorable name...Where did it come from? "It's a term my husband uses a lot," said Mallory. "Like he says 'That's my good stuff. Don't throw that away.' It means better quality—like fine wine is called the good stuff." I love it.

CRANBERRY ALMOND MUFFINS

**1 1/2 cups flour, sifted
1/2 cup sugar
1 teaspoon baking powder
1/4 teaspoon baking soda
1/4 teaspoon salt
2 large eggs
1/2 cup butter, melted
1/2 cup sour cream
1/2 teaspoon almond extract
1/2 cup sliced almonds
1/2 cup whole cranberry sauce
pinch of cinnamon**

Mix the flour, sugar, baking powder, baking soda, and salt in a large bowl. In a separate bowl, beat the eggs; and add the melted butter, sour cream, and almond extract. Fold the liquid mixture into the dry ingredients. Stir until moistened. Batter will be lumpy. Fill greased muffin tins in the following layer method: batter, 1 tablespoon cranberry sauce, and batter. Top each muffin with sliced almonds. Bake in a preheated 375° oven for about 30 minutes or until tops are rounded and lightly browned. While the muffins are cooling, sprinkle with a bit of cinnamon.

Makes approximately a dozen regular sized muffins.

THE QUEEN ANNE INN
SOUTH BEND, INDIANA

"It all started with a muffin bake-off, believe it or not," said Pauline Medhurst. She and her husband are owners of the Queen Anne Inn where top billing goes to the historic atmosphere of the Queen Anne and Neo-Classical seventeen room mansion. The Medhursts, members of the local bed and breakfast association, were participating in a contest meant to promote awareness of their services. One of the muffin bakers, a lady named Jane, had a British husband and loved to serve afternoon teas. She offered to help launch a tea program at the inn.

In 1989, South Bend residents could partake in simple teas at the inn with scones, cookies, and tea; but in November of 1990, Pauline decided to amplify their tea service. She attended a seminar about serving teas at the Columbus Inn in Columbus, Indiana, and began to research Victorian teas. These days, each Thursday afternoon and one Saturday afternoon a month, a full-fledged tea is unfurled at the Queen Anne Inn. The tea time spread has a similar structure each week, but courses include an impressive repertoire of variance each week. There are always two or three kinds of scones, the cornerstones of afternoon tea. Some of the flavors you might expect to see include chocolate chip, currant, apricot, cinnamon, or almond. Lemon curd or jams are likely scone partners. The layered sandwiches are almost always a spread of egg salad and a second flavor such as chicken salad or corned beef for the other layer. The open-faced sandwiches are topped with vegetables such as thin cucumber or tomato slices. Several tea breads will delight the palate. Pauline rattled off a few: chocolate walnut, apricot nut, banana, zucchini, poppyseed, pineapple, or lemon flavors. She likes to try recipes. There's always the favorite chocolate chip cookies or a variation of that all-American recipe. Brownies and lemon bars are also two tea time staples with other sweets such as shortbreads or

English tea cakes rounding out the repast. Besides the finger-sized sweets, desserts are served as well. Pauline likes to dazzle guests with a lighter cake for tea such as lemon or raspberry torte or angelfood cake with fresh berries and cream. She's happy to supply a succulent fresh fruit plate, if given advance notice, for a dieter or diabetic guest. Hot teas that warm the soul year-round, and iced teas that extinguish the fire of hot weather complete the tea menu.

As in most Victorian mansions, there are a series of large common rooms that are sublime sanctuaries of tea time service. Pauline arranges seating vignettes in her formal living room, music room, and dining room. Each place is set with silverware and a cup and saucer. Tea is poured chair-side, and guests are invited to pass through a buffet line to collect their choices. Pauline has thought about many other types of service, but this seems to be what her guests like best. If she has a smaller group of ten or twelve, they will be seated in the dining room (used as the inn's breakfast room with the hand-painted, silk wallpaper that is original to the house. "We pour their tea, they pass the food, and we try not to bother them too much," she said.

She likes to play cassette tapes with soft classical music or to provide live music on special occasions.

Children aged three and older are welcome anytime there's tea at the inn. It's a place for conversation and for children to learn about appropriate conversation. Pauline enjoys watching the mothers and daughters. She said tea time is a very special time for mothers and daughter to share time together. Young girls often are dressed in white gloves and shoes.

Special teas for children are held several times a year. Often, story tellers from the library will provide entertainment. A Santa Claus tea complete with you-know-who is scheduled for Christmas time this year.

South Bend is an interesting place, and the Queen Anne Inn is within walking distance of sites within the historic district. It

South Bend, Indiana

would be a good idea to enjoy tea at the mansion, check in, and spend some time seeing the sights. The downtown Century Center, (designed by Philip Johnson), The Tippecanoe Place Restaurant (an 1889 house built by Studebaker that is now an exquisitely restored fine dining place), the Studebaker National museum, and the wonderful Oliver House Museum (Copshaholm—with 38 rooms and furnishings from the 16th to 20th centuries) are all within short walking distance. The University of Notre Dame and St. Mary's are just a short drive. The Queen Anne Inn has a historical tale itself. The bookcases in the library were designed by Frank Lloyd Wright, and the mansion was moved onto the site to save it from demolition a few years ago.

Pauline has an incredible insight into the psychology of tea time. It's enjoyable to listen to her philosophies on this make-believe-of-a-grown-up-kind event because she makes me even more secure that promoting tea time is a worthwhile project. She views tea as a "finer thing of life." She said, "Tea is like taking the world into stock. Tea has always been considered a time for chatting with friends. It's very therapeutic." She said that some regular teatotalers have a favorite place to sit, and that some people like to come alone to spend time writing and having quiet time.

The inn is also well known for its specialized wedding services including intimate bridal teas, small weddings, and receptions.

Victorian atmosphere, quiet tea times, and a fine selection of tea treats are woven together to produce this fine tea room tale. Tea at the Queen Anne Inn will be remembered as a time where genuine hospitality flows like butter and honey on a warm biscuit. Queen Anne (and Queen Victoria) would surely approve.

EASY LEMON TEA BARS

1 cup flour
1/4 cup powdered sugar
1/2 butter
2 eggs
1 cup sugar
2 tablespoons flour
3 teaspoons grated lemon rind
1/2 teaspoon baking powder
2 tablespoons lemon juice

In a large bowl, combine the 1 cup of flour and powdered sugar. Using a pastry blender or two knives, cut in the butter until mixture is coarse crumbs. Press the crumb mixture into the bottom of a 8 or 9-inch square pan. Bake in a preheated oven for 350° for 15 minutes.

Combine the eggs and sugar in a small bowl. Blend well. Stir in the 2 tablespoons flour, lemon rind, baking powder, and lemon juice. Pour filling over the partially baked crust. Return to the oven, and bake 18-25 minutes or until light golden brown. Cool completely, and sprinkle with powdered sugar, if desired. Cut into bars of the desired size.

South Bend, Indiana

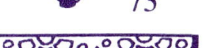

LEMON CURD

4 tablespoons unsalted butter
1/2 cup sugar
1/2 cup fresh lemon juice
4 egg yolks, slightly beaten
1 tablespoon grated lemon rind (optional)

Combine the butter, sugar, lemon juice, and egg yolks in a heavy saucepan or double boiler. Over low heat, stir and cook the mixture until it thickens enough to coat the back of a spoon. Do not boil (it will curdle). Remove from heat, and stir in the lemon rind. Pour into a jar and refrigerate.

Serve lemon curd on warm scones, over fruit, angelfood cake, or ice cream. It will keep for up to two weeks in the refrigerator if tightly covered.

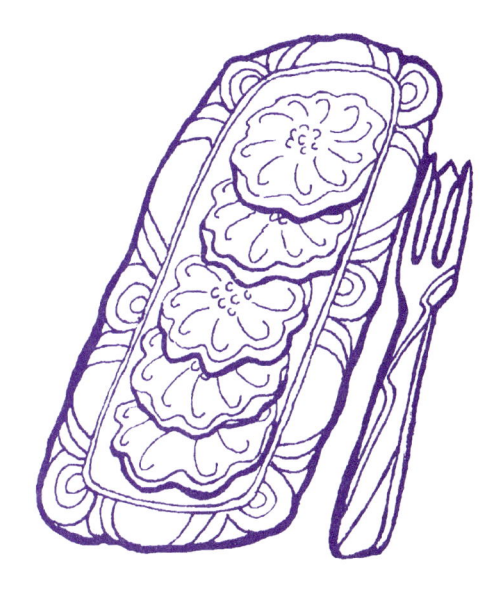

THE ROSE ARBOR TEA ROOM
MISHAWAKA, INDIANA

A rumble of voices from the second level of the building interrupted my perusal of the enticing display of English country antiques in Antiques, Etc. in historic downtown Mishawaka. I spotted the sign at the bottom of the stairs for the Rose Arbor Tea Room and proceeded carefully up the stairs to view a sea of diners having a gay old time. There were tables of ladies playing bridge, others wearing hats, and many were zestfully splurging on irresistible desserts. They were clearly enjoying themselves to the fullest as they took their pleasures in this beauteous tea room.

Carol Brademus, owner of the Etc. decorating shop (a block down the street), also owns Antiques, Etc. Thirty dealers specializing in American Country, Victorian, English Country, designer accessories, rugs, and children's apparel are clustered under one roof. Her plan was to have a four-table tea room where desserts, coffee, and teas were served. She dedicated the second story space to this endeavor. "The whole thing fell into my lap," said Lynett Heritz who operates the tea room. Her cousin told her to go down to take a look at "the old gas building" where he was showing his antiques. Lynett had been doing catering, had waitressing experience, and was looking for a job where she could work for herself. Carol needed someone to handle the tea room end of her business. "So I looked at it, said it was cute, and went home. My cousin told me to go look again. I ended up looking at the place six times. Each time I looked longer and thought a little harder." She knew she would have to serve more than beverages and desserts to generate enough sales to keep the tea room afloat. She told Carol what she had in mind, and the Rose Arbor Tea Room literally bloomed into a full-fledged luncheon room. "The day I opened, we had seventeen guests; and it just grew and grew," she said.

Mishawaka, Indiana

Mrs. Brademus used her expert decorating knack to carve a tea room out of the second floor of the old building. Wallpaper with a single rose bud motif covers the top part of the walls, and a pink plaid paper serves as a chair rail on the lower section. Antique accessories from her home decorate the walls including Victorian prints with fetching, gilted frames. A large, open, china sideboard is filled with rose and white transferware china and is topped with cascading silk flowers and stacked hat boxes. Located near the tea room entrance, is a tea cart loaded with a three-dimensional display of cakes, cheesecakes, and other desserts. An old framed restaurant plaque above the kitchen door reminds Lynett and her staff to "Serve a Good Dinner" (it's working). The addition of some seasonal silk flowers and clay flowerpots with silk plants for table centerpieces complete the garden theme and coordinate with the rose-patterned china dishes.

Lynett described her best selling dishes as the grilled chicken and spinach salad (see the spunky, hot raspberry vinaigrette dressing recipe to follow); the marinated tuna and vegetable plate with potatoes and green beans in a zesty herb vinegar and oil dressing topped with tuna, tomatoes, eggs, etc.; quiches; and the Rose Arbor turkey Philly with gourmet quality smoked turkey breast, cream cheese, cranberry-orange relish, and sprouts on multi-grain bread. Salads and quiche are served with a homemade muffin. A cold soup and a hot soup are offered each day in the warm weather. Cold quesadilla soup was one of the day's soups when I visited. It is milder than gazpacho with chunks of cucumber, green pepper, and onion with a yogurt and sour cream base.

Cheesecakes are her specialty, and everyone seems to know it—the double chocolate cheesecake which was the day's special was gone by the time I was ready for dessert. Actually, its absence was kind of a blessing. There were less choices to stew over as I tried to make my selection. There was a gooey, fudgy, Mississippi mud pie, chocolate-peanut butter cake, yellow cake with coconut buttercream frosting, and a chopped apple cake with caramel sauce draped over top. Sometimes I think a tea room mandate requiring desert sampler plates in all tea rooms would be an excellent idea.

The drink menu is jazzed up with the addition of Italian sodas—a gladsome combination of sparkling water and a touch of cream served with your favorite flavor over ice: almond, apricot, cherry, kiwi, hazelnut, passion fruit, raspberry, strawberry, or vanilla. In addition to regular coffee and tea, there are gourmet flavored coffees and iced coffees, espresso, cappuccino, chocolate cappuccino, and flavored latte—a serving of espresso with steamed milk, topped with a small amount of foam and tinged with some luscious flavors. A special kind of tea is available each day, and Lynett is not afraid to experiment with flavors such as hibiscus or anything else she can find that seems enticing. Sometimes she goes as far as her herb garden for chamomile or peppermint teas.

Mishawaka is just minutes east of South Bend, Indiana. Notre Dame University is close at hand, as is the northern Indiana Amish country and the famous weekly Shipshewana flea market and auctions (where up to twelve auction rings run at one time). The Indiana Dunes and Lake Michigan areas are less than an hour away. The Beiger Mansion Inn, a neo-classical limestone mansion with gourmet dining, is a block up the antique store-laden street from the Rose Arbor Tea Room. (See the Queen Anne Inn chapter for more sights in South Bend.) There are many recreational opportunities and unique bed and breakfasts in this area which is located on Interstate 80.

Lynett projects a sense of contentment with her work and an excitement for working for herself. She's very grateful for the help of her mother-in-law who helps her man the kitchen and is a principal baker in the operation. The ladies have their work cut out for them. It's a big job to make a place where their customers will make time to stop and smell the tea room roses. Well done, ladies.

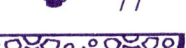

ROSE ARBOR RASPBERRY VINAIGRETTE

1/3 cup pureed fresh or frozen raspberries
1/3 cup raspberry vinegar
2/3 cup walnut oil (or mild vegetable oil)
2 teaspoons Dijon mustard
1 teaspoon fresh thyme (1/2 teaspoon dried)
1/2 teaspoon fresh rosemary
salt and pepper, to taste

Combine all ingredients, and whisk together. The dressing ingredients will separate on standing. Shake before use. Keep refrigerated.

Lynett says she experimented to get the combination that is stronger in flavor than many the raspberry vinaigrettes. She recommends that readers experiment with their favorite herbs to customize the recipe to their tastes.

GRANDMA'S ANGEL FOOD CAKE

1 angel food cake mix
1-20 ounce can crushed pineapple, undrained
1-3 ounce package vanilla pudding mix (not instant)
1 pint whipping cream
1/3 cup chopped maraschino cherries

Bake angel food cake according to package directions and cool. Mix the pineapple and pudding mix in a heavy medium saucepan. Cook over medium heat, stirring constantly, until very thick. Remove from heat. Cool and chill well. Split the angel food cake into 3 layers. Whip the cream and fold into pineapple mixture, and add the chopped maraschino cherries. Spread generously between the layers and on the top of the cake. Keep refrigerated until ready to serve.

This recipe came from Lynett's mother. Lynett could never get it to come out right until her mother told her the secret— use a boxed mix for the cake. (My mother gave me the same advice.) It's a really simple recipe but is a big favorite at the Rose Arbor, and customers ask for the recipe.

THE STORY INN
STORY, INDIANA

If you decide to venture to the Story Inn for tea, you'd be well off to pack an overnight bag—you'll want to stay. Maybe you should pack two bags—you'll want to say a long time.

The inn's focal point is its tin-sided general store, rebuilt after a fire in 1916 to include a second-floor Studebaker assembly area. The general store is definitely on the rustic side, and it will capture the hearts of all who enter. There's a decrepit liar's bench on the front porch and a pair of old gas pumps with blown glass crowns. As you step to the front door, you'll feel the boards spring underfoot; and you'll be aware that many work boots must have hit that very spot over the store's colorful history. Inside, is a huge pot-bellied stove plus lots of old general store shelving, and memorabilia. It feels like the store owners abandoned the place one day, and someone wandering through the woods found it years later. The sense of history oozes from the floor cracks and condenses off the tin ceiling.

The general store has been renovated into an inn for over 15 years; but owners, Gretchen and Bob Haddix, are newcomers. They purchased the inn in early 1994 from Cindy Schultz and her husband, Benjamin, who had expanded the inn's boundaries to include all the buildings of the late 1800's boom town except for one house. Family obligations necessitated their move, but they kept the inn until they found buyers they deemed acceptable to carry on the inn's traditions.

Small cottages serve as guest houses and make the inn a thirteen unit venture. Gretchen had grown up in Indiana, and she and Bob were anxious to get back to the Midwest. They moved from their country home in New York when their children were grown.

Robin Smith, pastry chef and old-time staff member, has been appointed the director of afternoon tea at the Story Inn which is available in the dining room or screened back porch. "People come here to splurge," she said. Don't expect a light, delicate fare. In the mid 1980's, the *Indiana Monthly* magazine named her turtle cheesecake as the best dessert available in the state; the award put the Story Inn's dining room on the map. "I originated my version of turtle cheesecake before the market was wild with it. It has a caramel and chocolate crust, a chocolate ganache layer, crushed pecans, and a flowing layer of caramel over top. We use good quality ingredients here, and we don't skimp on anything. The cheesecake became our earmark. Sugar cream pie is another favorite. It's requested over and over. I can't believe what I make is that special to people, because I love doing it," said Robin. She said some people ask to be seated next to the old-fashioned, oak, bakery case so they can see the desserts while they enjoy their meals. It's quite a view. Robin's raspberry chocolate torte, another favorite, was featured in *Midwest Living* magazine.

Afternoon tea has always been available at the inn—the sign out front announces the tea hours to be from 2:00 to 4:00 on Tuesdays through Sundays. One of Robin's goals is to upscale the inn's service by adding their own herbal honeys and butters and more bite-sized dainties. Gretchen is a tea aficionado who likes to offer teas you won't find in the grocery store or even in most tea shops in the Midwest. Ginseng tea is one of her favorites. She also likes strong black teas, herbals, and Chinese varieties. She's always on the look-out for exclusive lines and finds tea-timers like to experiment.

Robin presented my husband and me with a large, oak-rimmed, tea tray with tea for two. The tray was decorated with French leaves and included a large plate of dipping crackers and shortbreads such as anise buttons, almond sticks, and maple logs made with whole oats, grains, brown sugar, and honey. All were quintessential tea time treats, rich with buttery goodness.

Gretchen and Bob are erecting several old log cabins within the town to act as additional guest cottages. They will blend in

Story, Indiana

with the other authentic cabins that dot the "hollers" along the winding road to Story. A surrounding state park mercifully protects Story's hills from commercial ventures and billboards. A local artist is sculpting a tree across the road from the inn to depict the story of Story.

Nashville, Indiana, is Story's mailing address. It's a resort town with plenty of entertainment opportunities and over 350 shops. Bean Blossom is just up the road from Nashville—home of the legendary father of bluegrass music, Mr. Bill Monroe, and his yearly music festival which draws from 50,000 to 100,000 people each year.

But it really doesn't matter what is located close to the Story Inn. Once you get there and experience the peace, you'll be hard-pressed to leave. It was chosen as Indiana's best inn in 1988; and thank goodness, things aren't known to change quickly in this neck of the woods.

ROBIN SMITH'S SUGAR CREAM PIE

1-9 inch prebaked pie crust
4 cups heavy cream or half & half
2 cups granulated sugar
6 tablespoons cornstarch
1/2 cup lightly salted butter (no substitutes)
1 tablespoon lightly salted butter, melted
Whole nutmeg for grating
1 teaspoon vanilla—pure, of course

Combine cornstarch with sugar until well mixed in small bowl. In a heavy saucepan, pour in the cream; and whisk the sugar mixture in until well blended and no granules appear. Cook over medium low heat, whisking constantly to keep mixture from settling into the bottom of the pan and scorching. When the mixture thickens and pulls slightly away from the edges of the pan—remove from heat and drop in the stick of butter and allow it to melt while stirring occasionally to incorporate. When combined, add the vanilla, mix well and pour into the prebaked pie shell. Smooth the top of the pie, and drizzle the one tablespoon of melted butter over the top. Grate a good sprinkling of fresh nutmeg over the surface, and place under a hot broiler for 1 or 2 minutes until the nutmeg and butter mixture forms a glaze. Watch carefully. Most broilers vary in temperature.

Robin adapted this old-timey recipe from the Shakers. "The Shaker version isn't rich enough for me. I really like the texture. It's great if you like creamy things. This is the recipe people ask for a lot."

THE TEA ROOM
ELKHART, INDIANA

"What does a former opera singer do after studying, performing, and teaching in Europe with her tenor husband?" reads the menu of the Tea Room in the heart of Indiana Amish country. Janet Myers graciously shared her version of the correct answer to that question.

In 1978 she and her husband were back in the States, living in Elkhart, her husband's home town. On her birthday, he gave her $500; and she decided to use the money to open a store with "goodies, antiques, and four tables" on Bowery Street. She concentrated on baking European pastries from the many recipes she'd collected in Europe, and the recipes continue to delight customers today.

The tea room was close to Miles Laboratories, and soon many business people began to flock to the shop. When they asked for sandwiches, Jan added a roast beef sandwich on homemade bread. Then she added ham sandwiches and soups from her European recipe collection. "People lined up," she said. "It was so much fun!" She said even the tables and chairs were for sale. "We'd sell their chairs right out from under them."

Then the city began to renovate the area. They tore up the street and parking lot. Jan needed to make a change. She was saddened at the thought of closing but didn't know what to do or where to move.

Cindy Donnellon, a young, part-time waitress, was appalled that the Tea Room might meet its demise. "I kept thinking 'It has to work. It's too good not to work,'" she said. She offered a loan to keep the Tea Room afloat. Mrs. Myers graciously declined the offer but promptly asked Cindy to become her partner. It was the fulfillment of a dream for Cindy, an eighteen year food service veteran. She'd always wanted to own a restaurant. Now she's a partner and manages this lovely tea room that specializes in "unique cuisine, private dinners, old-world pastries, and our original recipes." At Cindy's suggestion, they relocated the tea room to its current home at the Greencroft Tower on Main Street.

Blue Willow and flow blue china pieces are the tea room's decorating signature. Many attractive blue and white china groupings are showcased throughout the tea room. A tea set given to Mrs. Myers by her grandmother is on display. Regular customers have given Jan some of the pieces from their homes, and others find pieces such as tea pots which they present to her. "They want to be a part of it," she says. Other decor includes antiques (she pointed out an unusual round white enamel pie safe hanging on the wall that says 'Give us this day our daily bread' in German) and old framed menus from the ship Queen Elizabeth's dining room and European restaurants.

Mary Ellen Strong, Jan's sister, is a willing set of hands in the kitchen. She's baking tempting coffee cakes and strudels each day before 5:00 a.m. (ouch). She also is the master of the European yellow egg bread that is the staff of many of the tea room's most popular dishes.

Irresistible, made-fresh pastries include raspberry or blueberry cream cheese filled coffee cakes; apple, cherry, and peach strudel; and cinnamon, pecan, or cheese rolls. All are habit-forming accompaniments for a nice "cuppa" your favorite herbal tea or beverage.

Sandwiches are often served on Mary's egg bread with mild horseradish, and the tea room is still known for its original roast beef sandwiches. A smoked salmon plate is listed on the menu as a "special taste to please you." Thinly sliced Oregon smoked salmon cream cheese and lettuce are served on a flaky croissant with a lemon dressing on the side that would be good with the salmon or the fresh fruit accompaniment. Other favorites are the chef salad with tea room dressing, spinach Greek salad, and homemade soups.

Pastries don't stall on the breakfast menu. Special renditions

Elkhart, Indiana

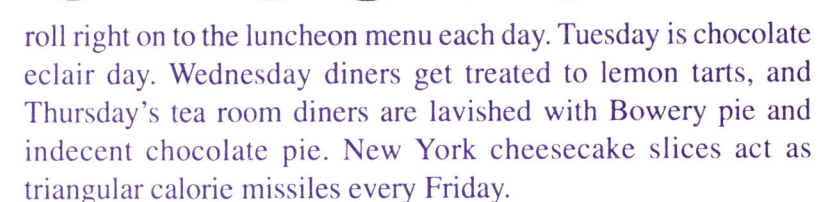

roll right on to the luncheon menu each day. Tuesday is chocolate eclair day. Wednesday diners get treated to lemon tarts, and Thursday's tea room diners are lavished with Bowery pie and indecent chocolate pie. New York cheesecake slices act as triangular calorie missiles every Friday.

The Tea Room is located on the first floor of a building that holds a collection of other businesses. The upper floors are occupied by retirement housing residents. Guests stream down from upstairs, their visitors in tow; and business people often grab tables for impromptu meetings. Many of the guests are like family, but the tea room has notoriety around the world. In November of 1989, it was featured in *Gourmet* magazine.

Cindy has maintained a high reverence for the food that is created in the Tea Room's depths. The others poke fun at her. "It's an art. I'm still afraid to handle the food (it's so beautiful)," she says.

I didn't get to visit long enough in the Tea Room. On my trip to this part of the world, I spent an hour scouring literature and doing tea room detective work before retiring, but I did not find a single tea room lead. I awoke the next morning and decided to try again. When I picked up a brochure from the top of last night's stack, it fell open to an ad the size of a postage stamp for the Tea Room (love that name). I stared in disbelief. I already had two appointments that day, but I was unable to pass up visiting the Tea Room. When I arrived, it was shortly before lunch—the worst possible time to pay a surprise visit in my vivid memory of food service experiences. That opera training must create nerves of steel. The two ladies took the little time they had to share their history, thoughts, recipes, and made me feel welcome.

Now you know what a former opera singer does after studying, performing, and teaching in Europe. She shares her talents with her tea room family, is immortalizing her recipes in print by writing a cookbook called *Tastes from the Tea Room*, and helps to make a young woman's dream come true. All I can say is God bless her!

BOWERY PIE

1 9-inch pie crust, unbaked
1 cup white corn syrup
1 cup brown sugar
3 eggs
1/3 cup butter, melted
1 1/2 cups pecans
1- 4 ounce milk chocolate bar, divided in squares

Evenly distribute candy bar squares on the bottom of unbaked pie crust. You will have about 8 squares left. Blend the corn syrup, sugar, eggs, and butter. Add the pecans and pour on top of the chocolate squares. Bake in a preheated 350° oven for 45 minutes or until pie is set.

This pie is named after the beloved Tea Room on Bowery Street. Jan doesn't tell us what to do with the leftover chocolate squares. Does anyone venture a guess?

NEW YORK CHEESECAKE

1 cup all purpose flour
1 stick butter
1 egg yolk, beaten
1/4 cup sugar
1/2 teaspoon grated lemon rind
1/2 teaspoon vanilla
4 eggs
2 egg yolks
1/4 cup whipping cream
1/2 teaspoon grated lemon rind
1 3/4 cups sugar
1/2 teaspoon vanilla
1/4 cup all purpose flour
5-8 ounce packages cream cheese, softened

Mix flour, butter, egg yolk, and sugar together with lemon peel and vanilla into a ball of dough the consistency of pie dough. Press enough of the dough onto a springform pan to cover the bottom. Bake in a preheated 400° oven for 8 minutes. Remove. Place spring pan ring around the bottom crust and secure. Press the rest of the dough on the inside ring. Pat dough evenly to make a side crust for the cake.

Mix 4 eggs and 2 egg yolks, whipping cream, lemon rind, sugar, vanilla, and flour in a large mixing bowl until smooth. Add softened cream cheese. Beat well. Pour into the spring pan. Place in oven at 450° for 15 minutes. Turn temperature down to 325°; and bake 45 minutes more, or until a thin knife inserted in the cake comes out clean. Remove from the oven. Cool 10 minutes. Remove outside ring.

This is the Friday dessert feature at the Tea Room. They recommend adding your favorite topping.

THE TROLLEY CAFE
GOSHEN, INDIANA

A trip to the Old Bag Factory complex with its Trolley Cafe is a one-stop Hoosier experience. Built in 1890 to house the Cosmo Buttermilk Soap Company, a maker of fine bathing soaps, the old manufacturing structure was the starting point for Goshen's trolley system from 1896 until the 1930's. Inside the main entrance, old trolley switch plates continue to reflect an era gone by. The trolley tracks remain intact and run the length of the building in what is now a garden. From 1915-1982 the Chase Bag Company occupied the three-story structure.

In 1984 Larion and Nancy Swartzendruber purchased the site and launched their Old Bag Factory restoration project. Swartzendruber Hardwood Creations occupies a good portion of the main floor. Here, Indiana native hardwoods are drafted into fine, custom-built furniture. Their showroom is an integral part of the Old Bag Factory's draw, and an observation balcony allows visitors to witness the furnitures' construction.

There's nothing high falutin' about the Trolley Cafe, but the tea room is of a much higher caliber than most eateries in tourist or shopping centers. It's owned by Aaron Hoober, a banker of seventeen years and a missions veteran of twelve years for the Mennonite church. Aaron had reached a point in his life where he wanted to work in a business of his own. He wasn't certain what kind of business, but when the opportunity for a turn-key sale of the Trolley Tea Shoppe presented itself, it seemed to mesh well with the other facets of his life; and he decided to purchase the tea room.

Aaron calls himself the tea room "go-fer" guy. He works in any area he sees a need and especially likes to welcome customers. His country-style friendliness makes certain the tea room remains a place where hospitality abounds.

Luncheon sandwiches are served on gutsy slices of thick-

Goshen, Indiana

sliced, homemade bread and are served with chips or fresh, raw vegetables. The vegetables are an excellent idea, lend a colorful touch, and I'm certain many customers applaud their crunchy presence.

The soups are soups with virtue. The daily street car vegetable is about as down-home as you can get. Aaron says the chef's corn chowder is superb, and the Greek Lemon soup is an interesting selection. All are served with a slice of French bread. (Homemade, European breads are one of the cafe's specialties.)

Vegetable quiche and quiche Lorraine, omelettes, and a children's menu are available as well as a couple of special entrees such as a chicken Waldorf salad.

Please throw any intentions of skipping dessert at the Trolley Cafe to the Indiana wind. Besides their famous pies, cheesecakes, and poppyseed bread, Aaron makes his own sherbet. The strawberries with shortcake was a resurrection of a favorite dessert from my past. It was real shortcake—little heavy hockey pucks of baked dough—only slightly sweetened. It was shortcake with character—not the wimpy sponge or cake versions that soft, white-bread, city-slickers try to pass off as the real thing. It was served with creamy milk like it would be down on the farm.

Breakfast is a recent addition to the Trolley Cafe's offerings. Folksy, European Danish rolls are a hit; and homey baked oatmeal is served with raisin toast. Aaron says it's a recipe his wife got years ago from relatives in Pennsylvania who like to serve it. It is accompanied with milk to pour over the top. (See recipe to follow.)

The Trolley Cafe is a visual showcase in a quietly elegant country setting (which probably attributes to its popularity for private evening parties). The entrance is a Victorian porch replica complete with gingerbread moldings. The floors are wooden, and one long wall is made of brick. There's a round, stained glass window, photographs of scenes from this heavily Amish and Mennonite farming area, and wallpaper in muted shades of green and peach. But of utmost appeal to road-weary tourists are the beckoning rattan chairs.

The Old Bag Factory will continue to undergo renovations and additions of shops in the years to come. Preserving its historical character is a priority of the Swartzendrubers. Highlights of the complex are a potter's shop with a large studio where you may watch the potter throwing his clay, a working blacksmith's shop, and the most spectacular quilt shop I've ever seen. Quilt Designs is a two-story, 1837 log cabin full of original contemporary quilt designs with vintage roots that are pieced and quilted by Amish farm women. Of interest to tea lovers is the Secret Garden—an herbarium with cookbooks, herbs, teas, seasonings, etc. The Cameo Collection, with fine cards and gifts, has hand-carved cameos; and I noticed many gifts with a tea theme which I would have purchased in a flash if I was in the marketing stage of this book rather than the composing stage.

I guess I'll just have to make a return visit to the Trolley Cafe in a few months. Until then, I'll remember Aaron's wish for all of his customers. It's simply stated on his menus: "May our Lord Jesus fill you with joy and hope, and until we meet again, may He hold you in the hollow of His hand." Thanks, Aaron, and may the Lord continue to be with you.

Goshen, Indiana

BAKED OATMEAL

1/2 cup oil or applesauce or a stick of margarine
2 eggs
2 tablespoons baking powder
1 cup milk
1 cup brown sugar or white sugar
3 cups oatmeal
1 teaspoon salt

Mix the oil, sugar, and eggs in a medium bowl. Add the remaining ingredients, and stir until mixed. Grease an 8-inch by 8-inch baking dish, and fill with the mixture. Bake at 350° for 30 minutes.

Heat slices before serving, and serve with milk poured over the top.

Mary Jane Hoober collected this recipe from relatives in Pennsylvania. Although not native to that area, it has become one of their favorites.

POPPY SEED BREAD

3 cups flour
1 1/2 teaspoon baking powder
1 1/2 cups milk
1 1/2 tablespoons poppyseed
1 1/2 teaspoons vanilla
1 1/2 teaspoons almond extract
1 1/2 teaspoons salt
1 cup plus 1 tablespoon oil
2 1/2 cups sugar*
3 eggs

Combine ingredients. Beat 2 minutes. Bake in two greased loaf pans in a preheated 350° oven for about 50 minutes or until golden brown.
*If you prefer a less sweet bread, reduce the sugar to 1-1/2 cups.

GLAZE:
3/4 cup powdered sugar
2 tablespoons butter
1/2 teaspoon almond extract
1/2 teaspoon vanilla
1/4 cup orange juice

Poke holes in bread with a fork, and pour glaze over the bread while bread is still warm.

This recipe was graciously donated by Erna Bachman.

THE VICTORIAN GUEST HOUSE
NAPPANEE, INDIANA

When you leave your job of fourteen years and your husband sells the service station he's owned for twenty years (plus a farm) so that you can become full-time bed and breakfast hosts, you try real hard to make your new business work. It's been about two and a half years since Vickie Hunsberger took a different route to do some errands and spotted a real estate sign in the front of the historic Coppes mansion. After a year of soul-searching, discussions, and prayer, she and her husband, Bruce, purchased the town's grand landmark-turned-bed and breakfast home.

It took five years for pioneer cabinet maker, Frank Coppes, to complete the construction of the elegant house he began to build in 1887. Four generations of the Coppes family lived in the home until it became a guest home for Nappanee travelers that is decorated with antiques and original family furnishings. A bell that is still in the floor under the Jacobean dining room table was used to summon the family's servants. Original, stained glass windows were made by a man named Lamb who once produced his art locally. It is said his pieces rival Tiffany's glass in value.

Serving Sunday afternoon teas has been a way for the old house to work harder to cover its giant renovation and upkeep costs. The teas have also provided good opportunities to share the house with local residents.

Vickie devised a year-long tea schedule (she takes a break in the summer months) and advertised one time in a local newspaper. Each month she continues to promote her teas by placing a sandwich board in the front yard on tea week. Tea themes and dates correspond with each month's holidays or the season.

Tea seatings are scheduled for 2:00, 3:00, and 4:00 p.m. Vickie and Bruce, dressed in Victorian garb, welcome guests and ask them to be seated at the small furniture groupings in the double parlor and dining room. Each guest may make a choice between four types of teas. Tea service is provided in a collection of vintage tea pots, and guests are asked to help themselves to a buffet of tea treats in the grand dining room.

The buffet consists of small sandwiches, cheesecake (Vickie's personal domain), homemade truffles, and a variety of tea cookies created to match the month's theme.

Reservations are appreciated, and although limited due to space, walk-in guests are welcome. More than 50 guests often appear for tea.

Vickie has a small boutique of items she has made for sale which has items such as tee shirts, aprons, recipe packets, and Victorian Guest Home mugs in one corner of the parlor for craft lovers; and a tour of the six guest rooms is the perfect end to a perfect afternoon of tea.

Afternoon tea in romantic surroundings with tempting tidbits to nibble provokes a luxurious aura of escape from the modern world. You can't fail to be impressed by the relaxing feeling that is gained when you know you're treating yourself (and perhaps some guests) to tea time in a Victorian mansion.

Nappanee calls itself "a gateway to Northern Indiana's Amish country." The historic Downtown Nappanee District was placed on the National Register of Historic Places by the U.S. Government. The farmland surrounding Nappanee is occupied by the Amish, Mennonite, and German Baptist sects. Many of the farms remain as they have for years with no electricity, gas, or telephone lines. Black buggies drawn by horses have never been replaced by automobiles in some of these families, and many of the farmers don't use tractors. Amish Acres, one of Indiana's top tourist attractions, is a historic farm, theater, and a collection of restaurants and inns that amplify this simple lifestyle by historical interpretation.

Nappanee is accessible by the Amtrak line that runs from Chicago to New York. The Hunsbergers are happy to shuttle guests from the vintage 1908 station to their inn, and the downtown area

Nappanee, Indiana

with its many antique shops is only a few blocks from the Victorian Guest House. The Borkholder Dutch Village, a relaxed version of today's shopping centers, has hundreds of antiques and crafts booths plus auctions, shops, and restaurants and is just a few miles away.

I plan to high-tail-it back to Nappanee as soon as possible. It looks like a good area to explore when I'm on a less rigorous schedule. These tea room tours are just teasers that whet my taste for more of the Midwest's fine countryside.

Vickie and Bruce use their fine home as a tool for ministering to their guests' needs—not just as a Victorian showcase. Their genuine Christian love radiates through all they do for their overnight and tea time guests. Their brochure declares their motto through mention of a Bible verse in I Corinthians 13:13 (...and the greatest of these is love) and alerts guests that they should "Prepare for a Memory" at the old Coppes Mansion.

CHOCOLATE CHIP CHEESE CAKE

2 tablespoons butter, melted
2 1/2 cups chocolate cookie crumbs
2 pounds cream cheese, softened
2 cups sugar
4 eggs
1 teaspoon flour
1 teaspoon vanilla
1 cup sour cream
1 cup mini chocolate chips

Make a crust by mixing the melted butter and cookie crumbs. Press in the bottom and up the sides of a well greased 10-inch springform pan. Combine the softened cream cheese, sugar, eggs, and flour. Mix until smooth. Add vanilla and sour cream until just blended. Stir in chocolate chips with a spatula or wooden spoon. Pour over crust in springform pan. Bake in a preheated 325° oven for 60 minutes. Turn off the oven, and open the broiler door (or leave door open a crack if you have an electric range). Leave cheese cake in oven for an additional 30 minutes.

Glaze:
3/4 cup chocolate chips
1/4 cup butter

Melt the chocolate chips in a microwave or over a double boiler, and stir until smooth. Spread on the cheesecake. Refrigerate.

IOWA

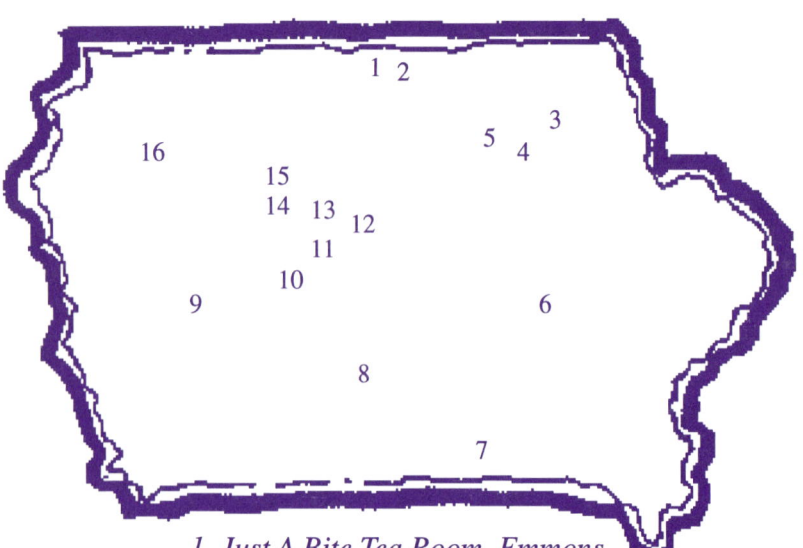

1. Just A Bite Tea Room, Emmons
2. Cottage Sampler Tea Room, St. Ansgar
3. The Country Porch Tea Room, Hawkeye
4. Diekman Mercantile, Denver
5. The Brandenberg, Waverly
6. Emma's Tea Room, Williamsburg
7. One of a Kind Bed & Breakfast, Tea Room & Gifts, Centerville
8. Bette Dryer's Tea Room and Catering, Indianola
9. The Owl House, Walnut
10. Thymes Remembered, Perry
11. The Barkley House Bed & Breakfast, Boone
11. The Douglas House Tea Room, Boone
12. The Blue Onion Tea Room, Roland
13. The Carousel Tea Room & Bakery, Story City
14. The Blue Willow, Harcourt
15. Tea Thyme at Sadie's, Fort Dodge
16. Martha's Coffee Station, Cherokee

THE BARKLEY HOUSE BED & BREAKFAST
BOONE, IOWA

An 1893 two and a half story house, resplendent with Victorian details, is home for Rosella and Dave Hanson and is an exciting alternative for Boone travelers who crave something more than an ordinary motel room stay.

Tea at the Barkley House is full of indisputable charms because service is provided by the owner who also prepares the food from a menu tailored to the occasion. Rosella is an exuberant party planner who specializes in designing tea parties and showers for up to thirty people in the open floor plan of the old mansion. Tea is served on a reservation-only basis for groups of ten or more.

Stained glass windows in the Barkley House are kaleidoscopes of colors woven into magical, transparent tapestries. The Hansons have borrowed their bold color scheme of rich teal, raspberry, and grape tones from the windows which are found in nearly every room.

Rosella started collecting Victorian antiques, china, and serving pieces when she graduated from Iowa State University and became a home economist. She liked to spend weekends picking up the bargains that she now uses in her tea services at auctions.

The three guest rooms at the Barkley House have private baths and are just as lovely as the downstairs foyer (with original, working gas lamp), dining room, library, and parlor. I could just sit in this house, breathe deeply, and attempt to inhale its beauty. The wood, antiques, colors, and glow of the stained glass windows makes it one of the most beautiful places I can remember being in. I wanted to luxuriate in its splendor. Rosella, Dave, and their daughter have living quarters in the former ballroom of the third story.

Guest breakfasts are titanic. I got a chance to test Rosella's culinary skills as I enjoyed the chilled strawberry soup, cheesy

The Barkley House Bed & Breakfast

hashbrown breakfast casserole, muffins, and scones. Tantalizing treats are her homemade red wine and champagne jellies that she produces for gift shops and serves at teas.

Rosella's a scrapbook lover, like me, so I was fascinated as I looked at her memory album of teas she's hosted. An example of a menu she's devised follows. I can't help but believe that anyone's guests wouldn't feel special to be served such a fine tea time spread.

Tea Time at the Barkley House
Chilled Strawberry Soup
Currant Scones with Butter Rosebuds
Ham and Cheese Swirls
Cheese Spread on Pumpernickel Stars
Chocolate Shortbread Hearts
Queen Victoria Sponge Cake
Petite Cheesecakes
Tea or Coffee

In the Douglass House Tea Room chapter, I expounded on the historic railroad attractions in Boone, but there are other things to see near or in Boone. There are several museums, the Iowa Arboretum (a library of living plants), Iowa's only guest ranch, and plenty of antique shops. It's only fifteen minutes to Ames and Iowa State University's concerts and sporting events. A twenty minute drive will get you to Story City where you can view or ride the historic carousel with its hand-carved animals (see Carousel Tea Room chapter) and find bargains at the VF Outlet Mall. Forty minutes away is Des Moines with Living History Farms, Valley Junction shops, the Governor's Mansion, and much more.

When people ask me to name my favorite tea room, they're really not playing fairly. Like my friends, tea rooms are special for different reasons. The Barkley House is special for its atmosphere and because the Hanson's hospitality is first rate.

CHILLED STRAWBERRY SOUP

4 cups strawberries, washed, stemmed, pureed
2 cups sour cream or plain yogurt
1/2 cup powdered sugar
1/2 cup white wine

Whisk all ingredients together in a medium mixing bowl and serve. Makes 12-1/2 cup servings

CREAM SCONES

2 cups flour
2 teaspoons baking powder
2 tablespoons white sugar
1/2 teaspoon salt
6 tablespoons butter
2 large eggs, well beaten
1/2 cup plus 1 tablespoon heavy cream, divided

Sift flour, baking powder, sugar, and salt into a medium mixing bowl. Cut in butter until the mixture resembles coarse crumbs. Make a well in the flour mixture, and add eggs and 1/2 cup cream. Mix with a wooden spoon until dough begins to form a ball. Then knead with your hand in the bowl about 30 seconds. Do not over-knead. Turn dough out onto a lightly floured surface, and cut in half. Form each half into a ball, and flatten to form a circle about 3/4 inch thick and five inches in diameter. Cut each circle into eight wedges. Place wedges one inch apart on a lightly buttered baking sheet. Brush tops with remaining cream, and sprinkle each with coarse sugar crystals. Bake in center of preheated oven 12-15 minutes at 425°. Makes 16 scones.

BETTE DRYER'S TEA ROOM AND CATERING
INDIANOLA, IOWA

"You can't train someone to be the best cook. There has to be a natural talent," said Harry Dryer, Bette Dryer's husband and support team. Although Bette's training was in the field of elementary education, she has used her natural culinary talents to capture over 1000 ribbons at the renowned Iowa State Fair cooking competitions—where the best of the best engage in head-on kitchen battle. She's won countless county contests, as well as those sponsored by government commodity groups and nationally known food companies. In 1987, she swept three of five categories (light and lean, ease of preparation, and overall winner) at the National Beef Cookoff. Actor James Garner, spokesman for the Beef Council, was in the audience to witness Bette's landslide win. Her beef fillet supreme recipe netted $34,000 in prizes and caused the rules of the contest to be changed the following year to limit one prize per participant.

After years of success in food competitions, Bette started a catering service. Six years later she began to search for a building that would be suitable for wedding receptions, special events, and a tea room. The building Harry found did not meet her specifications. It was a dark, dirty, old bar, and she told him she'd move back to Florida if he leased it. He did, and she didn't. Harry tackled the first remodeling project of his life to produce a suitable building for his wife's endeavors. She refused to set foot in the place for months until he needed her opinion for final decorating.

The ambience of the tea room is above reproach, but it does not resemble a Victorian tea room that some tea room lovers might expect. Harry's fine collection of Maxwell Parrish-era prints line the walls producing a gallery effect. The couple has been collecting antique china and other decorating accents for years, choosing pieces for individual uniqueness and beauty rather than as part of a collection of related items. It's a fresh look. Periwinkle blue

Indianola, Iowa

velvet chairs from an old St. Louis hotel slide under tables set with mismatched china and clear or colored glass dinnerware. There are several vintage buffets and an old upright piano draped with a tapestry shawl—complete with aging sheet music for any guest with a notion to play a few licks. An old street light that once cast its light over the Missouri governor's mansion has been trimmed to room size. It welcomes guests in the foyer and has become Bette's logo. The overall look of the tea room is eclectic and old world-like. It appears to be Victorian at first glance. A second look will dispel that theory.

Bette's food is also a bit apart from normal midwestern tea room fare. It's a collaboration of her colorful gourmet creations and easy recipes using convenience foods. She has developed the following philosophy: "You can try to improve on some products made with mixes and the like, but you'll never be able to do it—so why beat yourself up?" She laughed as she said, "They call me the Cool Whip Queen." Instead of using real whipped cream which easily separates (especially annoying in competition cooking), she suggests mixing non-dairy topping with a little sour cream for consistency and flavor. She said that she once asked a panel of five professional judges to compare real whipped cream with her concoction. Three of the five judges thought hers was the dairy product.

The tea room menu includes at least one hot and one cold entree each day with suitable accompaniments. Meals prices include soup, beverage, and the dessert of the day. An example of a fine meal served here might be: cream of carrot soup, baked breast of chicken with Dijon sauce, saffron rice, winter vegetable salad, tea breads, and Ozark apple pudding.

Everything is homemade and well seasoned. Bette uses liberal amounts of herbs and smaller amounts of liqueurs to create flavors with depth and sparkle. Although nothing is over-seasoned, all the food I tasted was far from bland. Bette is considering writing a cookbook because she sincerely enjoys sharing what she's taught herself about her craft. She admitted the process will be difficult because she often uses no recipes and may never make a dish the same way twice. However she makes it—it will be good!

Her community minded spirit won her the city's Golden Hammer award for business excellence last year. She enjoys working with other businesses on projects. A recent Mad Hatter's Tea Party was a sell-out with a long waiting list and was a collaborative effort with four other entrepreneurs. Guests were invited to wear their "maddest" hats to a special luncheon, style show, and program.

Indianola is located in a prime location just 12 miles south of Des Moines and 30 miles east of Madison County's covered bridges. Each summer the town hosts the National Balloon Classic (hot air balloon competition) and is home to a balloon museum. Simpson College, a private establishment, is located here. The Des Moines Metro Opera, with one of the finest reputations in the country performs in Indianola at the college for six weeks each summer. The performers of the entourage frequently dine in the tea room. Bette says that once in awhile a pianist will perform on her old piano, and opera members will stand to sing their parts.

Bette must believe in "truth in advertising." I was privileged to listen to her entertaining radio show one day when she told listeners "Everything at our tea room is fresh and homemade. I think you'll find a bit of difference at our tea room. We have gourmet food and offer special services. Remember, if you settle for less than the best—that's what you'll get!"

Indianola, Iowa

PRIZE WINNING GREEN APPLE RELISH

1 whole medium-sized dill pickle
1 whole Granny Smith apple, cored and unpeeled
1 Vidalia sweet onion
1/4 cup vinegar
2 tablespoon sugar

Place all ingredients in a food processor, and pulse on and off until desired consistency.

KEY LIME PIE

2-8 ounce packages cream cheese, room temperature
1 cup sour cream
2-14 ounce cans sweetened, condensed milk
1 cup lime juice (Key Lime juice is especially good.)
2-9 inch pie shells, baked

Blend cream cheese, sour cream, and milk until smooth. Add lime juice, and mix well. Pour into the two baked pie shells, and bake 10-15 minutes at 300°. Cool and refrigerate.

Makes 16 servings.

The baking time on this recipe seems short, but you'll be pleased with the results!

BEEF FILLETS SUPREME

4 beef tenderloin steaks, each 4 ounces
1 teaspoon lemon pepper
1/2 teaspoon cardamom
3 tablespoons butter
2 tablespoons wine
1 tablespoon soy sauce
1 teaspoon Dijon mustard
2 tablespoons sliced green onions
4 fresh mushrooms, thinly sliced

Mix lemon pepper and cardoman. Sprinkle over the fillets. Heat butter in a heavy skillet until very hot. Cook fillets 3-4 minutes on each side. Remove to heated platter. Add onions and mushrooms to skillet. Stir-fry 2-3 minutes. Add wine, soy sauce, and mustard, scraping the pan. Heat thoroughly, and pour over fillets to serve. Garnish with parsley. Serves four.

This is Bette Dryer's $34,000 National Beef Cookoff winning recipe. I have tried it and can attest that it's truly special.

THE BLUE ONION TEA ROOM AND GIFT SHOP
ROLAND, IOWA

"Yes! This is the old Midwest I remember." This was my thought as I drove into Roland, Iowa. Rows of pick up trucks surrounded the grain elevator which was large enough to cast a shadow over the entire town. Big, four-door cars were lined up in front of the neighborhood-style grocery store. The water tower was a prominent land mark. When I was young, I frequently wondered how water towers work. I still don't know, but I think it's one of those things you stop worrying about when you grow up.

Mary Ann Anderson, resident Norwegian and owner of the Blue Onion Tea Room, served me a delicious chicken casserole which was reminiscent of church cookbook cuisine—creamy and soul-warming. Lettuce salad and perfectly baked, homemade yeast rolls were the meal's comforting accompaniments. The Blue Onion's menu is a collection of salads, sandwiches, quiches, casseroles and desserts. It's all homemade, and you'll find the pastry selections to be the crowning glory of your meal. On the day I visited, there was coconut cream pie, pecan pie, praline ice cream pie, rocky road bars, sour cream with raisin bars, and Norwegian treats.

Settled by Norwegian immigrants in the mid 1880's, the town's heritage is reflected in the delicacies of the Blue Onion's pastry menu. Mary Ann delivered my kavring (melt-in-the-mouth, twice-baked sweet breads) and kringla twists and said, "You have to put butter on them. That's the way we eat them." I found them to be very satisfying because they were not too sweet. A nice sack-full would make a perfect gastronomic souvenir.

Honest, straight-from-the-heart hospitality has made the Blue Onion a popular central Iowa dining spot. Lunch at the tea room is like dining at the home of your favorite aunt except that all the knick-knacks are for sale. Mary Ann has a large following of

The Blue Onion Tea Room and Gift Shop

fans. She said she feeds bridge clubs, shower guests, business meetings, and church circles. She serves bus tours and theater buffs attending the nearby Nevada theater. Elderly people with no room to entertain at home bring their guests to the Blue Onion. Mary Ann is happy to serve a five to seven course high tea to groups of up to 40 with reservations. Homey meals featuring dishes such as pork chop or chicken casseroles or ham balls with sweet potatoes and all the fixings are her specialty.

In 1988 Anderson and three other women opened the tea room in an old tavern building. The tea room got its name from the classic Blue Onion china pattern they loved. Anderson still uses the china and the motif as a decorating theme. Crocks with stenciled Blue Onion patterns sit on each table to cradle crackers.

Fanciful tea pots are attention-getters in the gift area of the tea room. Other gifts include church and local cookbooks, Nordic sweaters, designer sweatshirts, china, stoneware, etc. Mary Ann is very choosy when she selects gift items for her tea room. She seeks hard-to-find items that will delight her customers.

Each year's highlights have been the spring and fall style shows that Mary Ann coordinates with fashion stores from Ames. The shows have expanded into two-seating events during each season. Mary Ann uses a different menu and music each year to provide variety for repeat attenders.

Roland is a few miles east of Story City (see chapter on the Carousel Tea Room) and is twelve miles north plus three miles east of Ames. It's surrounded by rich, flat, farmland and a great sense of serenity. Over 30 new homes have been constructed in the last two years—a real housing boom for a town of Roland's size.

I can see I'm not the only person that appreciates the town's quiet and charm. I concluded my visit to Roland with the feeling that the Norwegians know how to do it right. Garrison Keillor, wasn't fibbing.

Roland, Iowa

UGLY DUCKLING CAKE

1 package yellow cake mix
2 eggs
1-16 ounce can fruit cocktail, undrained
1/2 cup margarine
1/2 cup white sugar
1/2 cup brown sugar
1/2 cup evaporated milk
1 1/2 cups shredded coconut

Mix cake mix, eggs, and fruit cocktail in a large mixing bowl with a wooden spoon or spatula. Pour into a greased and floured 9" by 13" pan. Bake at 325° for 45 minutes or until done. Cool.

In a medium saucepan, melt the margarine. Add the sugars and milk. Bring to a boil. Boil for 2 minutes. Remove from heat, and stir in the coconut. Spread the warm frosting on the cake.

Mary Ann says this is great as a coffee cake or served warm with ice cream.

THE BLUE WILLOW TEA ROOM
HARCOURT, IOWA

"Have you been to the Blue Willow in Harcourt?" I'll bet I was asked that question more than fifty times when talking to Iowa people about tea rooms. I was beginning to get a complex and wished I'd scheduled an appointment there when I first started my year-long tea room vendetta. What had I missed?

On the map, Harcourt appeared to be in a rather isolated part of the state with few tourist attractions. My lightning-quick mind deduced that the Blue Willow must be very special to create such a pilgrimage point for all the people I'd met who claimed to have been there.

The reputation of this famous eatery is so grand that I was a bit intimidated by the thought of asking Connie Gustafson, pioneer and creator of the tea room for an interview. Several people have been so inspired by the Blue Willow that they've taken the leap into the tea room business. I reminded myself that my over-active imagination is often more of a hindrance than a help. It was an honor to meet Connie for high tea one spring day and a sojourn of tea room fellowship. She's a gracious hostess who doesn't put on airs, which I greatly appreciated.

"I didn't know what I was doing when I started," revealed Connie. "I'm not quite sure where I got the idea. I'd never been to any tea rooms. I think I read something that intrigued me. Although, when people came to my house, we always did tea or coffee; and I would always do things a little fancy. This was back in the days when I didn't work. Maybe part of it came from that. It was always a good feeling to do that for somebody and just sit for the afternoon and enjoy each other."

The Blue Willow shares its building with the other part of Connie's venture—Country Treasures Gift Shop. The businesses are located one-half mile east of Harcourt on the farm that is her husband's birthplace. Rollie still farms the land, and his mother

Harcourt, Iowa

lives in the farmhouse next to the shops; while Rollie and Connie live in the metropolis of Harcourt.

About twenty years ago, her mother-in-law began searching for a way to fill her time, and Connie was a mother with young children at home. She'd previously worked in a office, transcribing records for medical histories. "We needed something to occupy our time, so we started the gift shop together. She was only in it for about five years. It was a teeny-tiny, little building, and the tea room is the fourth addition. The original building had been brought onto the property for the hired man to sleep in. So we both made things, and we decided we were going to sell them there, and it snowballed from the very first day we opened," said Connie.

About eight years ago, Connie unveiled her prototype tea room. She said the first day she opened, 50 people walked in and sat down. At that time, she was taking the orders and running back to the kitchen to fill them. "The first year I thought I was literally going to die from fatigue. I'd be here at nine or ten at night, and I'd come in at five in the morning to start baking. But you know, I think it takes that sincere desire to make it work and really hard work to make it grow."

"High tea is probably our very best," explained Connie. "Most people come to high tea thinking they'll get a cucumber sandwich and small desserts. This is patterned after the English country high tea." It's served at 2:30 in the afternoon and will probably satisfy your hunger enough to make dinner unnecessary. High tea at the Blue Willow is served in smaller portions than their hearty country lunches, but it has more courses. I counted seven courses on the menu, and a sorbet course was an added treat.

On the day I visited, the high tea menu was as follows:

The Blue Willow Tea Room

Orange Spiced Tea
Royal Berries
Creamy Vegetable Soup
Chicken Salad Gelatin Salad
Lettuce Salad with Lemon Glaze
Broccoli and Raisin Salad
Scones with Orange Butter
Chicken Parmesan with Noodles
Pastry and Sweet Variety Tray
Turtle Cheesecake
Peach Orchard Tea

The royal berries were a colorful mixture of blueberries, boysenberries, strawberries, and red raspberries. The salad variety plate included small samples of each salad. I found the lemon glaze lettuce dressing to be heavenly. Connie said she's been thinking of having it bottled for retail sale. The base dressing can be blended with salad dressing to serve over lettuce or with whipped cream to make it the perfect topping for angel food cake or fresh fruit. Chicken parmesan was a new addition to the high tea menu which constantly changes. Almond twists, sugar cookies, creme de mint brownies, and peanut butter brownies were a few of the dessert tray selections. (I always remember the chocolate ones.)

When Connie was a small child, there was a fire in her family's home. Only her teddy bear survived. Her original Blue Willow doll dishes were destroyed; but several years before the dining room opened a replacement set was discovered in an antique shop. It was very simple for Connie to decide on the name for her tea room, and she sometimes holds teddy bear teas for youngsters who tote their companions to tea.

Customers often spend many hours in the tea room and gift shop. "In Iowa, you have to drive quite a long way, and if you like it—you'll stay awhile," she said. Our server, Billie, explained,

Harcourt, Iowa

"They make a very special effort to come here. You can spend a day here if you want to pamper yourself." Some come for morning coffee, shop awhile, eat lunch, shop some more, and finally have afternoon dessert.

The Blue Willow is, of course, decorated in a blue and white color scheme. Many old linens are used to decorate the tables and walls. There's a sea of antique chairs, beamed ceilings, and plenty of floral wallpaper and borders. On the walls, are antique prints of English cottages with borders stenciled around them to add even more visual impact. You might have a relaxing time at the Blue Willow, but your senses will get an aerobic workout if you try to take in all the atmosphere.

Connie says tea rooms are very popular now because the baby boomers remember the homemade cooking in their pasts, but don't have the time to cook for themselves. We speculated about what will happen to tea rooms in a future generation when no adults can remember homecooking. It's a scary thought.

Many tea rooms have opened in Iowa since the Blue Willow set the pace eight years ago. Connie believes there is room for everybody—as long as each offers something very different from the next. She knows that customers can get bored if they encounter the same things at each one, so she constantly works at making changes to keep her tea room exciting.

A colossal salute is due Connie for her entrepreneurial spirit and leadership in the growing Iowa tea room community. It's clearly worth the special effort it takes to visit the Blue Willow where high tea is as much an event as it is a meal.

GINGERBREAD CAKE WITH PUMPKIN ICE CREAM

2 1/2 cups flour
1/2 teaspoon salt
1 1/4 teaspoon ginger
1/2 teaspoon allspice
1/4 teaspoon nutmeg
1 teaspoon cinnamon
1 1/2 teaspoons baking soda
1/2 cup softened butter

1/2 cup sugar
1 large egg
1 cup molasses
1 cup water
3/4 cup brown sugar
3/4 cup butter, melted
1 1/2 cups hot water

Combine the flour, salt, spices, soda, and set aside. Cream 1/2 cup butter and sugar until sugar dissolves. Add egg, and beat until well mixed. Add flour mixture alternately with molasses and water. Pour batter into 9" x 13" pan and sprinkle with brown sugar. Combine melted butter and hot water; carefully pour over batter. Bake for 40 to 55 minutes, or until cracked on top slightly. Serve warm with pumpkin ice cream.

Pumpkin Ice Cream:
1/3 cup firmly packed brown sugar
1/2 teaspoon cinnamon
1/4 teaspoon nutmeg
1 cup cooked pumpkin
1 quart slightly softened ice cream

In large bowl, stir together all ingredients except ice cream. Add ice cream by large spoonfuls until well blended. Spoon mixture into 9 inch pan. Cover, and freeze at least 3 hours.

*This recipe is taken from the **Blue Willow's Sweet Treasures** cookbook featuring the best of their high tea desserts, tea room antecdotes, and a collection of memories over the 20 year history of the Country Treasures Gift Shop. The pumpkin iced cream makes it extra special. Doesn't it sound like a comfort-food?*

THE BRANDENBURG
WAVERLY, IOWA

Owner, Cindy Shipman, says she didn't plan to have a tea room. She called her new business an "eating establishment" when she opened the Brandenburg in November 1992. Soon her customers began labeling the Brandenburg as a tea room, and customers are always right.

In 1886 the Brandenburg family started a jewelry business that was moved to the current tea room's building in 1911. The appearance of the building remains much as how it would have looked then. The Brandenburgs customized the jewelry store by constructing mountainous, glass-faced, oak cabinets on the two long walls. The cabinets are embellished with carved, wooden swags and wreaths which were popular motifs of the day. The tin ceilings are very high to accommodate the counter-weighted glass doors that open by raising straight up. There's an original oak screen door (it even slaps shut like the old doors used to) with a blue and white enamelware plaque denoting a jewelry association, and the ceiling lights are original—as is the wooden floor. A watch repair area near the door still has the oak cabinet with small drawers for watch parts. The sign above says "Not Responsible for Work Not Picked Up in 30 Days." Cindy remembers playing with a friend (the Brandenburg's grand-daughter) in the store when she was a tyke. She remembers that it was a very dark place where lights were switched on in an as-you-go basis.

The early 1900's atmosphere is so authentic that I felt like I should have worn my hair in a snood or some of those pointy Victorian shoes. Heavens knows—a Victorian corset would never do. It would take a modern, bionic girdle to cinch my waist down to the size a Victorian maiden would be proud of after this tea room tour.

When Cindy opened her eating establishment, she added a few of her own touches but was careful to stay consistent with the original decor of the building. She purchased Victorian-styled dining room chairs when the old Jesup Opera House furnishings were sold and has hung lace curtains at the windows. Antiques that are for sale are displayed in the store-front windows and old cabinets.

The menu is more extensive at the Brandenburg than at most tea rooms because as Cindy says—she didn't start out to be a tea room. A full breakfast is served six days a week and includes homemade cinnamon rolls. Luncheon selections include a menagerie of 16 sandwiches, two quiches with homemade muffins, a special casserole or stir-fry, soups, and desserts. Cindy stresses that everything is homemade. The sandwiches are available on whole wheat or white bread that is baked in the Brandenburg's kitchen. She also pointed out that every effort is made to reduce fat and cholesterol in her recipes. However, dessert lovers: You're on your own in the calorie counting department! Chocolate silk pie is a customer favorite, and I noticed piece-after-piece of coconut cream pie leaving the safety of the kitchen.

Special dinners are Cindy's favorites. Many guests had reservations from last year for this year's Valentines dinner. Each lady received a flower, and musicians from Wartburg College entertained guests. Entrees included a choice of baked salmon filet with cucumber and dill sauce, French seasoned pork loin rack, or Cornish hen with wild rice stuffing. A choice of soup or salad, twice-baked potatoes or yams contreau, mini loaves of bread, and Japanese blend vegetables accompanied the main dishes. Also included were angel hearts with almond sauce and red raspberries plus complementary wine. The meals are priced as a good value to customers, and the Brandenburg is a great place to entertain business or special guests.

Waverly (population 8,444) is the county seat for Bremer County. It's also the home base for the well-known Star Clipper dinner train. Wartburg College is located there; and the University of Northern Iowa, in Cedar Falls, is less than a half hour's drive.

Waverly, Iowa

Waverly is home to the largest horse sale in the nation two times each year. People from all over the world attend to buy, or sell, or just to witness some of the best horse trading in America. I've heard it's a spectacular show.

Cindy tries to spend as much time as possible with her customers. She says, "I want to give them the best quality service they can possibly get. I like the bottomless-cup theory." Treating customers well is a good business practice, but I got the idea that Cindy doesn't do it just because of that. She genuinely likes people and likes to do what she can to make their lives more enjoyable.

With her attitude about hospitality, the authentic Victorian atmosphere, and homemade food—it's no wonder so many customers have rightly named her "eating establishment" a tea room. It's a lovely old-fashioned place—in every way!

THE CAROUSEL TEA ROOM
STORY CITY, IOWA

"I just winged it," said Candy Anderson. A love of special food and the desire to own her own business propelled her into the tea room business after fourteen years of working as a legal assistant. This was over four years ago. She'd expected to serve 35 or 40 customers a day when the Carousel Tea Room opened, but the figure doubled immediately.

Candy says the strong Scandinavian heritage of Story City attracts many visitors. No kidding! I'd never spent any time in this part of the state, so I was taken aback by all the ethnic indicators. They've got the Grand Viking Hall, the Sons of Norway Lodge, a Scandinavian restaurant with a Scandinavian buffet, and several Lutheran churches to pick from. I thought I'd crossed the northern Iowa border and entered the land of the happy Holsteins.

The Carousel is one of Iowa's more bustling tea rooms. At lunch time, it's operated on a no-reservation basis; and you may have to spend a bit of time waiting (which is not so painful if you're expecting it).

As in many tea rooms, the Carousel is noted for its chicken salad plate served with fresh fruit a tea basket (an assortment of Scandinavian breads and pastries). Homemade soups are also a big hit.

Scandinavian high tea is served at 2:30 p.m. Monday through Saturday with a 24 hour advance reservation. It's billed as "a four-course dining experience." Candy gave me a tour of the Carousel's high tea menu. It starts with fruit suppe and Kavring (cold soup and Norwegian bread crisps) and is followed by a cream soup. The entree course is generally something such as chicken puff pastry with lingonberries and mixed green salad with red grapes, pecans, and raspberry vinaigrette dressing. Finally, the awaited dessert sampler with rice pudding and three or four ravishing finger-sized pastries is presented. A different tea is selected for each

Story City, Iowa

course, to complement the flavors of the foods. There may be many participants in high tea, or occasionally there are none; but they are happy to serve tea to two or more guests with reservations.

Free-standing carousel horses; the red, white, and blue color scheme; lace, and Scandinavian decor enable the Carousel Tea Room to capture a look of its own. There's a large assortment of gourmet coffees, teas, and food to take home as well as Scandinavian gifts. Or you could make them happy at home with a big sack of baked goods. Candy said they have customers from Minnesota who make monthly bakery runs to the Carousel.

Story City is located just a couple of miles west of Interstate 35 in the center of Iowa, near Ames. At last count, fourteen specialty shops line the streets. Each is very different from the rest because shop owners work together to promote diversity and to plan numerous special events. The shops boast a significant lack of souvenir items and concentrate on featuring quality gifts.

Besides the tea room, the town's largest draw is Iowa's only operating carousel (hence the name for the tea room). It's been protected by a sheltering building since its renovation in 1982 and is open daily for viewing and riding from Memorial Day weekend through Labor Day weekend or by appointment from May through October (call 515-733-4214). The carousel has 29 wooden, hand-carved figures, and a 1936 Wurlitzer Military Band organ in the center which plays calliope tunes. There are 20 horses and two each of the chicken, pig, dog, and chariot figures plus a whirling tub.

There's also a historical opera building in Story City that has operated continuously for over 75 years. On a more modern level, a new outlet mall that attracts shoppers by the bus-load.

One more time, I am able to present a tea room success story. Candy took years of unrelated work experience and mixed it with her love for food and the desire to operate her own business. She whipped it all together and added lots of labor to develop a sparkling tea room in a state with plenty of competition. That's the way to "wing it," Candy!

ORIENTAL SPINACH SALAD

1 pound spinach, washed, chilled, and torn
1-8 ounce can water chestnuts, drained and sliced
1-14 ounce can bean sprouts, drained
2 eggs, hard-cooked
1/2 pound bacon, cooked crisp and crumbled

DRESSING:
1 small onion, minced
1/2 oil (vegetable or your favorite)
1/3 cup sugar
3 tablespoons vinegar
1/2 cup catsup
1 tablespoon Worcestershire sauce

Mix dressing with electric mixer and chill. At serving time, mix salad ingredients, and top with dressing. Serve immediately.

Story City, Iowa

KRINGLA

1/2 cup margarine, softened
1 cup white sugar
1 large egg
1/2 teaspoon salt
1 teaspoon soda
2 teaspoons baking powder
2 teaspoons vanilla
1 cup buttermilk
3 cups flour

Cream the margarine and sugar until creamy and sugar is dissolved. Add egg, salt, soda, baking powder, and vanilla; and mix well. Alternately, add buttermilk and flour (1/3 cup buttermilk and then 1 cup flour; repeat until all is incorporated into the batter). Mix well. Freeze dough overnight or up to one week.

Measure one teaspoon of dough onto a floured surface. Flour hands, and lightly roll into a rope shape about four inches long. Twist opposite ends of rope towards center to form "figure eight" shape. Bake on ungreased cookie sheet about eight minutes at 375°.

Yields about 3 dozen.

THE COTTAGE SAMPLER
ST. ANSGAR, IOWA

"The chicken is especially spectacular! The rice is right out of this world!" This was an easy one—I didn't need to think of a way to describe the food at the Cottage Sampler. The exclamations flying from the nearby tables filled in all the blanks.

A day at the Cottage Sampler Tea Room and Home Sweet Home Gift Shop is a day to savor. Judy Goplerud presides over the Cottage Sampler, and its name is an apt description for the cottage-like house on St. Ansgar's main street. An enclosed front porch, complete with Victorian screen door and menu blackboard welcomes guests to the 10:45, 12:00, and 1:15 luncheon seatings. The wallpaper is a clean navy and white ticking stripe. Tin folk heart napkin rings encircle the linen napkins, and the tables are clothed with navy and white homespun fabric. Other table appointments include ecru lace placemats, pistol handled serviceware, and stoneware crockery ice carafs. A teapot gallery borders the ceilings of the two intimate dining rooms, and there are several china cupboards filled with blue and white pottery that is for sale. There's a lot to look at in a small amount of space. The look is cramped, cluttered, and fresh—all at the same time and is orchestrated chiefly by the simple color scheme. Cozy is a word that sums up the Cottage Sampler very well.

In 1984, Judy opened Home Sweet Home—the gift shop on property adjacent to the tea room. "It was a 'turning forty thing,'" said Judy. She'd been a farm wife for many years, but was not just the lady who cooked the meals—she was one of the farmhands. When her son became of age, Judy discovered she'd raised a replacement for herself. In 1990 Judy decided to add the tea room her customers were asking for. "It just kind of happened," she said and swears she'd never intended to get into the restaurant business, but the house next door was for sale and perfect for a tea room. Her loyal crew is comprised of many friends who are

St. Ansgar, Iowa

also farmer's wives. Her daughter, Kari, and sister, Sheri, are regular helpers.

My elementary school-aged nephews accompanied me to the Cottage Sampler last summer. There was a chorus of "Where's the burgers?" when the waitress recited the menu. Their mother was worried that we should have stopped for fast food on the way to St. Ansgar. The boys enjoyed their smoked turkey croissants, deemed the honey Dijon sauce as "weird" and wolfed down their fresh fruit cups topped with a light, fruit-flavored custard. They experience their virgin voyages into the world of cheesecake as they shared a piece of the chocolate chip and were anxious to try another variety.

The tossed salad that is often served with entrees is a combination that will set your tastebuds to the tingling stage. Lettuce is topped with fresh strawberries, grapefruit sections, and a fruity homemade poppyseed dressing.

Judy says the menu is in a constant state of revision, but the chicken and seafood dishes are favored. Entree examples include chicken and crab Baltimore in puff pastry, seafood pasta salad, and chicken Wellington—a contender for the best entree I've ever eaten (recipe to follow). Special sandwiches and homemade soup are always available to the less adventuresome. A wicked list of homemade cheesecakes top the desert menu (raspberry, lemon, turtle, cookies and cream, etc.). Cakes are a customer pleaser, and I can attest for the tempting quality of the buttercream cake with coconut filling. Flavored coffees, teas, iced and hot cappuccinos, as well as many other beverages are available. A house specialty is the spiced raspberry tea that is brewed in the kitchen. Afternoon desserts and beverages are always available.

As appealing as the food is, Judy admits that people usually don't come just to eat. They come for the homey, comfortable feeling the tea room lends its guests. The Cottage Sampler is a very popular and well-known place. You could play tea room roulette and take your chances on getting a seat. However, reservations are highly recommended on Saturdays and during the summer months. Summers are special at the Cottage Sampler because the bricked patio area becomes an outdoor cafe.

St. Ansgar is located on the Highway 9 shortcut to Rochester, Minnesota, near the center of northern Iowa. It's not near a lot of major attractions, but it doesn't need to be—it's an attraction by itself.

On my recent departure from the Cottage Sampler, I noticed that country music radio stations lined the radio dial. A song about TLC and R&R for U and me summed up my experience at the Cottage Sampler quite well as I left town feeling pampered, content.

CHICKEN WELLINGTON

1-6 ounce package long grain and wild rice mix
Grated orange peel from one orange
1 tablespoon fresh parsley, chopped
Seasoned salt, to taste
Pepper, to taste
6 chicken breasts halves, boneless and skinned
1 egg white
1-10 ounce package frozen patty shells,
   defrosted in refrigerator
3-4 tablespoons milk
1-12 ounce jar red currant jelly
1/2 teaspoon Dijon mustard
1 tablespoon orange juice
2 tablespoons white wine

Cook rice mix according to package directions. Add the parsley, seasoned salt, and pepper. Let cool. Pound the chicken breasts to flatten slightly, and sprinkle with salt and pepper, if desired. Beat the egg white to the soft peak stage, and fold into the rice mixture. On a floured surface, roll the patty shells into 6-8 inch circles. Place a chicken breast in the center of each patty circle, and top with approximately 1/4 cup of the rice mixture. Fold the sides of the patties in and fold up jelly roll style. Place the chicken breast rolls in a shallow baking dish with the seamed side down. Cover tightly, and refrigerate several hours or overnight. Keep refrigerated until time to bake. Preheat oven to 375°. Brush patties with milk. Bake for 35-45 minutes, uncovered. Cover with foil if pastry browns too much. Heat jelly slowly; and add mustard, juice, and wine. Serve chicken with warm sauce and additional rice, if desired.

THE COUNTRY PORCH
HAWKEYE, IOWA

When I was a child, I never dreamed I'd return to Hawkeye by my own will. Those were the days when an hour felt like ten hours instead of 15 minutes as it does now. And we spent many long hours in Hawkeye waiting as my father performed one of his frequent swaps with the local car dealer. Now that I'm more "mature" I realize he was just shopping like many men do—hashing over all the aspects of the deal, rehashing it all several times until the purchase is conquered. It's a good method, but it's an endurance test for spectators.

In 1987 Marilyn Niewoehner and Ruthie Smith purchased a house on Main Street in Hawkeye that could easily fit into a Grant Wood painting with its austere architectural styling, front porch, and white picket fence. The house is approximately 100 years old and hasn't changed a lot from the time it was built. In fact, some of the lighting fixtures are original and were installed when electricity was made available to Hawkeye residents. Seven layers of stripped wallpaper later, the Country Porch was ready for business; and the ladies' tea room dream became a reality.

I'd visited the Country Porch many times in its early days, but I'd moved from the area and hadn't been there for at least three years. My memories had dimmed, and I was unprepared for the charming tea room I rediscovered on a recent visit to my old haunt.

Two small dining rooms hold seven tables, an old, green, enamel cookstove, and several antique cupboards that are filled with antiques and gifts for sale. Walls are accented with simple wallpaper borders.

Many of the Country Porch guests are out-of-towners. The ladies told me that after an article appeared in the Cedar Rapids newspaper, people traveled up to three hours to have lunch at their tea room.

Hawkeye, Iowa

Marilyn and Ruthie say there are no particular customer favorites. Everything they serve is well received. There's a homemade soup each day, a casserole with salad and a muffin, a sandwich, and several desserts—including a variety of homemade ice cream flavors. It's a simple menu, but there is something to satisfy all tastes.

On a recent visit, I had a ham casserole with a gelatin salad and a cinnamon muffin. It wasn't gourmet food, but it was like Sunday-best food in an old-fashioned Iowa home. I normally don't care for gelatin (ie. funeral food), but their version was ambrosial. It tasted like it was flavored with apricot nectar and peach slices. For dessert, I tried the cookies and cream homemade ice cream. My mother took the Butterfinger dessert so someone had to do it! Mother was surprised when I raved about how good it was. She knows that I am rarely tempted by ice cream—even in the old days when we'd make it as a Sunday evening treat with the cream from our own dairy. She dived in for a taste, heartily agreed with my assessment, and pointed out they'd used an excellent quality of vanilla. The ladies confessed to using an imported vanilla from an Iowan herb company.

The cinnamon muffins reminded me of a recipe for French breakfast puffs that I've been laboring over with only a 1:4 success rate. Their recipe is much more reliable, simple to make, and has a velvet-like crumb.

The Country Porch carries gifts and antiques, but the ladies say that people mainly come to eat. Such good food is distracting to even the best of shoppers. However, one very good seller is their *Recipes from the Country Porch* cookbook. They've sold close to 1,000 copies, which is amazing for such a small tea room. Marilyn said so many people asked for recipes that they decided to offer the collection. I can guarantee you'll never have to wonder what to take to a potluck again if you're fortunate enough to purchase one of their cookbooks. A small section of cold soup recipes has sparked my interest and put me in the experimenting mood. I vote that more tea rooms follow their example and publish their own cookbooks.

Marilyn and Ruthie are loyal members of the Hawkeye Community Historical Club. The club has recently saved two 100 year old buildings on Main Street from demolition and created the Hurd Center which houses a collection of artifacts from Hawkeye families.

Hawkeye is just a little off the path that many travelers take as they travel to the far northeast corner of the state to see Effigy Mounds (an interesting arrangement of raised Indian burial grounds), Yellow River Forest State Park, Norwegian festivals in Decorah, and the little picturesque towns along the Mississippi River. A brochure at the Country Porch listed 20 antique and gift businesses in a 50 mile stretch along Highway 150, but I'm certain there are many more.

It's been about 30 years since the days I accompanied my father on his Hawkeye car dealing ventures. I wish I could steal back all the time I wasted then for naps now! I never thought I'd go back, but I didn't know about tea rooms like the Country Porch then. And, yes, the car dealership is still there—like a monument to my youth—right next door.

Hawkeye, Iowa

COMPANY CASSEROLE

8 ounces fine egg noodles, uncooked weight
3 cups chicken or turkey, cooked and diced*
1-10 3/4 ounce can cream of mushroom soup
1-10 3/4 ounce can cream of chicken soup
1/2 cup mayonnaise
1 cup canned mushroom pieces
  (8 ounce drained weight can—don't drain)
1-14 1/2 ounce can asparagus tips, drained
1 cup cheddar cheese, shredded
1 medium green pepper, finely diced
1/4 cup slivered almonds

Cook noodles according to package directions. Drain. Combine meat, soups, mayonnaise, and mushrooms. Mix gently. Put half the noodles in the bottom of greased 9" by 13" pan. Cover noodles with 1/2 of the asparagus tips. Top asparagus with 1/2 of the grated cheese. Cover cheese with 1/2 of the meat mixture. Repeat the layering process. Top the meat mixture with green peppers and almonds. Bake at 350° for 45 minutes.

*Canned tuna fish may be substituted for the chicken or turkey.

You may find more Country Porch recipes in the cookbook they published featuring most of Marilyn and Ruthie's favorites.

CINNAMON MUFFINS

1 cup white sugar
1/2 cup margarine
2 eggs
1 teaspoon vanilla
1 cup sour cream
1/4 cup milk
2 cups flour
1 1/2 teaspoons baking powder
1 teaspoon baking soda
2 tablespoons white sugar
1 teaspoon cinnamon

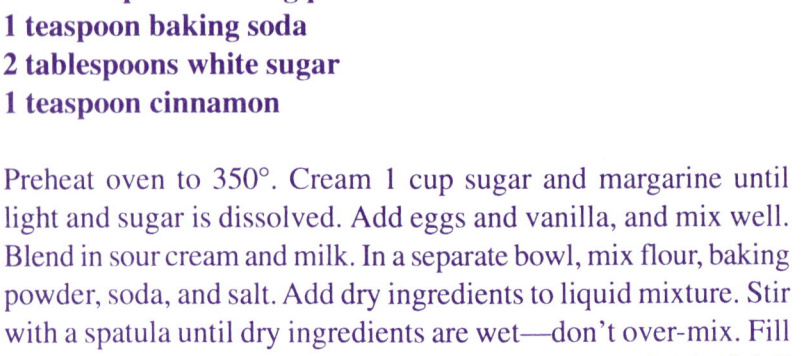

Preheat oven to 350°. Cream 1 cup sugar and margarine until light and sugar is dissolved. Add eggs and vanilla, and mix well. Blend in sour cream and milk. In a separate bowl, mix flour, baking powder, soda, and salt. Add dry ingredients to liquid mixture. Stir with a spatula until dry ingredients are wet—don't over-mix. Fill muffin tins with liners or greased (on the bottoms only) half-full of batter. Combine 2 tablespoons sugar and cinnamon. Top each muffin with approximately 1/2 teaspoon of the sugar mixture. Bake approximately 20 minutes or until muffins are rounded and lightly browned.

Makes 18-20.

These are my favorite muffins. They're moist and stay fresh for several days in the refrigerator.

DIEKMAN MERCANTILE AND TEA ROOM
DENVER, IOWA

Once upon a time, in a land not so far away, there lived a fair maiden named Marie who was also a pooped potter. She was extremely disheartened with the job of lugging her wares to and fro. Pots were so very heavy; and she wasn't getting any younger, you know. She wanted more than all the world to have a charming, little tea room of her very own.

When her knight in shining armor (tea room contractor, Steve) rumbled up in his blue, Chevy half-ton truck, he promised to help her with the nasty pottery drudgery if she would just marry him and move to the not quite a mile high village of Denver, Iowa. "It's a deal," said Marie. She locked her tea room dream in her secret treasure chest to be forgotten.

Soon, the happy couple was blessed with a flaxen-haired baby daughter, and Steve was busily constructing a castle for them deep in the woods of Denver Hills. Marie found herself becoming more and more melancholy as she spun more earthen vessels than ever on her potter's wheel. "When will it ever end?" she wailed. She was so very tired of dank clay and working in the musty, basement dungeon.

One day, Steve and Marie decided to venture out of the woods to travel to the big city of Chicago. They wanted to go to market to find merchandise they could sell with their pottery to lessen their work loads a bit. They only meant to spend the day, but they ended up staying a fortnight. They spent each evening with Marie's former lady-in-waiting (that's me) who lived in a high, brick tower with a fancy word processor.

On the way home, they talked and talked. Steve decided that Marie deserved to be granted her biggest wish in the whole, wide world—a tea room; and he even threw in a gift shop for good measure. "Oh, pooh!" said Marie. "I'll believe it when I see it." "No, really!" said Steve. "Your wish is my command." And within

Diekman Mercantile and Tea Room

a very few days, he found a building in their little village and proceeded to build Marie's dream. And that's how Diekman Mercantile on the main street of Denver, Iowa, got its grand start (with only minor modifications to make a better fairy tale).

Did they live happily ever after? It's a bit hard to say because they've only been open three days at this writing—but so far, so good.

All joking aside, Doug and I were very impressed by Steve and Marie Nowack's transformation of the dingy, unoccupied, old store front in Denver to its present status as the town's showcase. I had no doubts that Marie and Steve could do it. They are two of the most talented people I know. Formerly, the Diekman building had been a general store; and most recently, it had been a laundromat; so the job was a stretch—even for them.

The couple took the store's innate features: the tin ceiling, wooden floor, old pot-bellied stove, oak wall shelves, and safe, and added vintage store counters, seed bins, and Victorian architectural artifacts to create a look that will make you stop a few seconds as you step back in time and into this unique gift emporium. Marie says the three garage-fulls of old molding they purchased came in very handy in the decorating of the 3,000 feet structure. The wide front window is a whimsical garden setting which they will change with the seasons.

The place is loaded with collectibles, antiquities, confections, gourmet coffees and teas, pottery, folk art, and books; and of course the tea room is given a spot of honor— right inside the door. Tables with old sewing machine bases are topped with chintz, floral tablecloths. Chairs are painted, spruce green, antique and garage sale finds that Marie has been collecting for years—just for this purpose.

At this time, the menu is a variety of desserts and beverages from Marie's collection of recipes from family and friends. She is hoping to expand the menu to include full tea room fare in the future. On the day we were attentive samplers, the old child's

Denver, Iowa 133

blackboard listed pumpkin chocolate chip muffins, lemon thyme bread, cowboy coffeecake, peach creme cake, and summer delight dessert. Gourmet coffees and teas, iced tea, lemonade, milk, and soda were also available. The summer delight was a refreshing frozen dessert with a coconut cookie crust, nuts, whipped cream, raspberry and lemon sherbet. The lemon thyme bread was a recipe from a dear friend, Nancy Peters, who has been an inspiration to Marie and many herb lovers in the Cedar Falls area for years. Marie is anxious to start baking her mother's burnt sugar pie recipe which is not a common recipe in this part of the state, as well as her sugar cookies and molasses oatmeal cookies which were her childhood favorites. "They can't be topped," she said and looks forward to sharing them with her customers.

Marie said that she feels deeply indebted to all the friends who rallied to help them get Diekman Mercantile ready to open in such a short time. One lady decorated the front window, others helped arrange gifts, and yet another helped with the initial tea room baking and added a dozen homemade pie crusts for an opening gift. She also sewed the hems on the lovely tablecloths for the Nowacks. She'll never forget all their kindnesses.

Kindness—that's what tea rooms are all about. The moral of this story is: Don't keep your dreams locked up in your treasure chest—as Marie can testify, you'll never be able to forget them anyway; and use your kindness to help others make their fairy tales happen. Kind acts are so very much appreciated.

A Diekman update: The tea room is now serving luncheons six days a week and is known as the "home of the heart muffins." Marie says I need to see her herb bed. It's harvest provides the herb seasonings for many dishes. I don't get to visit often, but my mother keeps me informed. She says everything is "extra good." Marie invites you to see what Denver is all about. She says the quiche lorraine and curried turkey broccoli casseroles are two especially favored dishes, but not to worry, "It's all good stuff."

LEMON THYME BREAD

3/4 cup milk
1 tablespoon finely chopped lemon balm
 (use leaves and stems)
1 tablespoon finely chopped lemon thyme
2 cups flour
1 1/2 teaspoons baking powder
1/4 teaspoon salt
6 tablespoons butter
1 cup sugar
2 eggs, beaten
1 tablespoon grated lemon peel

Lemon Glaze: Mix the juice of 1 lemon and confectioners sugar to make a "drizzle."

Butter a 9-inch by 5-inch loaf pan. Heat milk with chopped lemon balm and thyme until hot. Allow to cool. Mix flour, baking powder, and salt in a small bowl; and set aside. Cream the butter, and gradually beat in the sugar in a medium bowl until light, fluffy, and sugar crystals are dissolved. Beat in the eggs (one at a time) until well blended. Beat in the lemon peel. Add flour mixture to the creamed mixture alternately with the cooled milk, mixing until just blended. Pour into the buttered loaf pan. Bake in a preheated 325° oven for approximately 50 minutes or until browned and a toothpick inserted in the center of the loaf comes out clean. Pour lemon glaze over the hot loaf. (You may want to reserve some of the glaze to garnish the slices as you serve them.)

This recipe will be of interest to herb lovers. It's a nice, moist texture. A fourth of a lemon slice and a piece of mint would be an appropriate garnish, as well.

THE DOUGLASS HOUSE
BOONE, IOWA

When the Douglass House was built in the 1870's, it was an Italianate showplace. It's one of Boone's oldest homes and one of the first homes in the nation that was wired for electrical service. A generator from a flax mill was switched on in the evenings to provide electricity for the home's residents. The slate roof is original to the house which was owned by the Douglass family from 1934 until 1991.

In May of 1991, Joleen (Jody) Meunch purchased the home and opened the Douglass House Tea Room after one mad month of sprucing up the old place.

Mamie Doud Eisenhower's family once lived nearby, and she and President Dwight D. Eisenhower were occasional guests in the Douglass House. Jody named the parlor-turned-dining-room the President's Room to commemorate this tidbit of the house's history. It has a high ceiling with an ornate plaster roundel, tall windows, and a generally elegant atmosphere. Two antique portraits that Judy purchased at the Douglass household auction decorate the walls. Other antiques in the room from the Douglass clan include a five legged oak table and the mantle from an old buffet. Yards of white lace swath the tables, and chair seats are covered in a burgundy colored fabric in the President's Room. The old floral carpeting was installed in 1956.

A second dining room is called the Green Room or Emmabelle's Room and has a lighter garden-look with white painted chairs that are fancied up with large attached floral, chintz bows. Old built-in cupboards were custom made many years ago for the house and shipped by rail from Illinois. Ruffled, chintz overcloths top forest green table coverings.

Three or four entrees are available each day such as Italian chicken puff, grilled Reuben and soup or the house chicken salad plate with dill, tarragon, and nuts (mine was so beautifully presented that I took a picture of it). Chocolate pecan pie is a favored dessert; but so that regular customers won't get in a rut, plenty of other tempters are ready such as scones, raspberry frozen yogurt, Inga's favorite pie (with coconut), chocolate dream cake, and cherry Amaretto amoré cheesecake.

Reservations are very much appreciated at the Douglass House because Jody's place is a participating tea room in the Iowa bus tour of tea rooms, and other special events are scheduled throughout the year.

The Douglass House's gift shop features clothing, accessories, bath shop items, and gifts. It's located in a portion of the downstairs of the house but is expanding heavenward to the second story, as well.

Carroll Street, home of the Douglass House, is one of Boone's most historic streets. The Mamie Eisenhower birthplace is there, and interesting gift shops in old homes flank each side of the Douglass House. Memory Lane has a huge selection of hard-to-find quilting fabrics and hundreds of craft patterns—many of them designed by the owner.

Boone's a good town to spend a day or night. There are beautifully appointed bed and breakfasts (see the chapter on the Barkley House) to stay in after a day of taking in the sights.

Boone's a railroad loving town. The Boone and Scenic Valley Railroad, which was formed in 1982, has 2,254 charter members—many of them with railroad workers on their family trees. Their goal is to become the best historic railroad in the Midwest. The train ride on the diesel train operates daily from Memorial Day through October 31 with a crew cast entirely of volunteers who love to share railroad stories. A Chinese-built, coal fed, steam locomotive called The Iowan operates on the weekends. The trains go over two trestle bridges high over the Des Moines River Valley, and the depot is not far from the Douglass House Tea Room.

One year I received a mystery adventure trip to Boone's train for my birthday. It was a long time ago, but I can remember

Boone, Iowa

stretching over the open passengers' car railing to get the best view of the river valley while my husband stood in the center of the car so he wouldn't get too close to the edge. We had a splendid time in Boone, and that was even before there was an inviting tea room like the Douglass House to make the trip even better.

CHOCOLATE DREAM CAKE

2 cups flour
2 teaspoons baking soda
1 cup white sugar
1/2 cup cocoa
1 cup water
1 cup salad dressing (not mayonnaise)
1 teaspoon vanilla

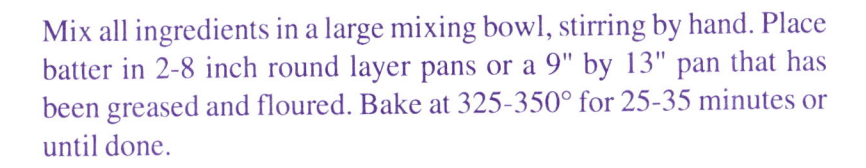

Mix all ingredients in a large mixing bowl, stirring by hand. Place batter in 2-8 inch round layer pans or a 9" by 13" pan that has been greased and floured. Bake at 325-350° for 25-35 minutes or until done.

Jody says this was always her children's favorite cake, but they liked it topped with plain white frosting. In the tea room, she likes to make it in layer cake pans. She spreads chocolate mousse between the layers and tops the cake with whipped cream and crushed Heath candy bars.

EMMA'S TEA ROOM
WILLIAMSBURG, IOWA

"Once we decided to call our place Emma's, everything seemed to fall into place," said Williamsburg sisters, Joan Heitman and Elaine Wartenburg. Emma, the ladies' mother who died over twelve years ago, is very much missed; and her memory is highly respected. "She could do it all," said Elaine.

There were six children in their family with four girls and two boys "in the middle." All of Emma's daughters enjoy cooking—especially baking. At home, everything was homemade. "We didn't even like homemade bread," remembers Joan in amazement.

When they opened their tea room on May 2, 1994, they helped to fill a great tea room void in eastern Iowa. I'd been watching that part of the state with a close eye—amazed that no one had realized the need for tea room dining.

"The local ladies encouraged us to open a tea room," said Elaine. Their reputations as fine country cooks were well known. Elaine had worked in a restaurant at the local country club. Their new tea room is located just a few miles south of the well-known Tanger Factory Outlet Center on Interstate 80, on the east side of the small town's square. The Picket Fence Gift Shop is located upstairs.

Although Joan never had previously worked outside her home, she was in intensive tea room training for many years without suspecting it. "I was a farm wife with a large garden. I did a lot of baking and canning and preserving. I especially liked the baking," she said. She now better understands the time pressures a woman working full-time faces and admits to having the need to order an occasional pizza when she gets home from the tea room.

All the food at Emma's is homemade using scratch methods. There are pies and cakes and sugar cookies—just like Mother's. An entree special, sandwich special, and Emma's Favorite are the main dishes. Emma's Favorite includes two homemade sandwich buns, slices of thuringer, a piece of yellow cheese and

Williamsburg, Iowa

one of white cheese, applesauce, and a sugar cookie. I was curious about how the combination was derived. They said their sister in Texas gave them the idea to have a trademark plate on a daily basis. They explained their mother liked summer sausage for a simple Sunday evening supper; she loved applesauce; and she was famous for her sugar cookies.

"They rave about the food here," said Joan. And on a recent visit, I deduced I'd be a fool if I didn't see why. Doug had Emmas's Favorite which included their signature homemade bread. There is no other way to describe that bread except as melt-in-your-mouth. And they'll bring you extra butterhorn rolls, if you'd like. The Fourth of July theme was carried forth with a special entree called Yankee Doodle macaroni which was a little casserole dish of plain macaroni, topped with spiced and crumbled ground beef, and garnished with sauteed mushroom slices. It was a take-off from an old dish their respective children loved on the farm and about as American as you can get. A patriotic garnishment of a red watermelon wedge, white butter rose, and a blue gelatin star made the dish even more special. Desserts included many pies (Toll House, coconut crunch, butterscotch meringue, lime meringue, fresh peach, fresh strawberry, and a colorful red, white, and blue pie). New York and butter pecan cheesecakes plus fudge cake rounded out the well-padded dessert list. I don't know about the other desserts, but the Toll House and coconut crunch pies had an even, fresh-from-the-oven, grandma-style warmth that no microwave could duplicate. Mint julep iced tea and butter pecan coffee were two of the day's delightful drink specials.

Setting up the business plan was the hardest part of starting their business, the tea room owners said. Their experience in tea room dining was limited. They'd planned to visit other tea rooms, but their opening deadline got in the way. "We lived in fairy land," said Joan. "We thought we'd do it all—but there's no way!" They have hired several retirement-aged ladies to help them serve, but Joan and Elaine plan to continue doing the part they love the most—their own cooking and baking. Joan says, "It's like waking up every morning and knowing company's coming!"

The tea room is located in the lower level of a building that was formerly a clothing store and is over a hundred years old. The tea room has an original stone wall, and is furnished with antiques. A large framed doily at one end of the room is one Emma crocheted, and there are old photographs of their mother as a child and in her adult years. A framed print with a verse entitled "Only a Mother" hung near our dining table. The color scheme is an old-fashioned blush of hollyhock pinks, white, and burgundy. The customers' appreciative comments about the appearance of the tea room add to the ladies' enjoyment of their work all the more. I noticed that people were as interested in introducing themselves to Joan and Elaine as the ladies were to meet their guests, and customers that did not know each other felt free to converse between tables. The servers were efficient, knowledgeable, and extremely welcoming. It was a good place to be.

It struck me that I've written about many tea rooms that are located just a few miles away from the section of Interstate 80 that runs through the Midwest. A few that come to mind (besides Emma's) are the Owl House in Walnut, Iowa; the Garden Room in Princeton, Illinois; and the Rose Arbor Tea Room in Mishawaka, Indiana. If you get a chance, pamper yourself a bit by stopping at some of these places to rejuvenate yourself on your travels. These tea rooms will be a gentle reminder to you to slow down a bit and savor life—two important things to keep in mind as you travel.

Williamsburg, Iowa

BUTTERHORN ROLLS

1 package dry yeast
1 cup warm water
1/2 cup margarine, softened
1/2 cup sugar
1 teaspoon salt
3 eggs, beaten
4 cups flour (approximately)

Dissolve the yeast in the warm water. Add margarine, sugar, salt, and eggs. Beat with an electric mixer until blended. Add two cups of the flour, and beat till smooth and satiny. Gradually add the rest of the flour, and stir until stiff. Then knead until a nice, soft dough forms. Place the dough into a large greased mixing bowl. Turn once so that top of dough is greased. Let rise in a warm place until doubled. Divide the dough into three parts. Roll each part to the shape of a square about 12 inches by 12 inches. Cut into 12 pie-shaped pieces. Starting with the wide side of each piece, roll into a horn, being sure to tuck the end of the dough to the bottom of the roll. Place on a lightly greased cookie sheet, and let rise till doubled. Bake at 375° for about 8 to 10 minutes. Brush the tops with butter. Makes about 36 rolls.

This recipe was given to me by Elaine Wardenburg. It is the wonderful signature bread at Emma's Tea Room. Watch for Elaine and Joan's cookbook that they are publishing. I'm hoping their recipe for potato chip sandwichs will be included. These ladies really know how to make good food.

JUST A BITE TEA HOUSE
EMMONS, MINNESOTA / IOWA

"It's your fault!" Bobbi Coulter pointed an accusing finger at her sister, Becky Aalgaard. She was referring to the story of how her family found its way from their California home to battle the Iowa climate in Emmons, a town of about 500 on the northern border.

When Becky was in high school, she dated a boy with relatives in Iowa. Later, she married one of the Iowan cousins. Four years after that, Bobbi decided to break loose from her frenzied California lifestyle as a vice president of an advertising company. She traveled a lot and worked long hours. "I was barely functioning. I was just exhausted. They used to tease me at the day care center because you had to have a list of people authorized to pick up your child, and Ryan's was two pages long," said Bobbi. Ryan was very fond of Becky's husband which helped prompt her move. "My decision was made after the Los Angeles riots. A car backfired in our neighborhood, and my son was scared because of what he'd seen on television. Then our father became sick. So we brought him and my mother out here. We took him to the Mayo clinic, and they fixed him up. He's doing fine now," said Bobbi.

She is now in charge of the advertising and promotional aspects of the family business. Becky is the tea room's accountant. She had previously worked at Treasured Moments, an Emmons crafts and collectibles store. She believed there was a large enough market in Emmons to warrant a tea room and knew traveling customers wanted a place to dine when they visited. Both ladies help their mother, Donna Hall, operate the tea room. Donna's special talents include office management and interior designing. A fourth family member, Becky's mother-in-law, does the baking.

This tea room is called a "tea house" because the tea rooms in their area of California were called that. Just a Bite was named by Becky's husband who noticed his mother-in-law always liked to

Emmons, Minnesota / Iowa

try "just a bite" of this and that when they went out to eat. He thought it would make a good name for the tea house. An apple with a bite missing cleverly became the tea room's logo, and foods are often served on glass plates shaped like apples.

A snappy menu of California favorites, adapted to midwestern tastes, is Just a Bite's fare. Each day they offer a special salad, sandwich, and luncheon plate selection which is called a "dinner" (accurately named because in the rural Midwest, the noon meal is often called dinner, and the evening meal is supper).

Sandwiches are often open-faced and broiled in the oven. Salads are served with homemade soups or muffins. Dinner entrees come with appropriate accompaniments and include variations of chicken or turkey breast or midwestern favorites such as ground pork and beef loaf with roasted potatoes.

The favorite dessert selection is the Just a Bite sampler plate. It's the size of a whole slice of cheesecake but consists of one third piece of three different flavors such as New York style with very-berry sauce, pecan praline, and double chocolate. The tea room is well known for its fresh peach pie, in season. People come in during the morning to reserve slices for an afternoon snack because they know it will be gone by that time.

They admit that planning menus with their Californian tastes for midwestern customers has been tricky. They were surprised at the passion for red meats in this part of the country. (White meat is the choice of Californians.) One time they served a dish using unfamiliar flour tortillas. A customer wagged her finger at them and said, "We **know** this isn't lefse!" Obviously, the Scandinavian influence is a big one in this part of the Midwest.

The ladies wanted to serve afternoon teas; but when the concept proved unpopular, they decided to try having teas at the lunch hour and have had great success. Customers look forward to the next tea. Each course is a variety plate of bite-sized portions. An appetizer plate, breads and spreads plate, main course sampler plate (examples: taco tarts, turkey and potato truffles, Hawaiian meatballs, ricotta-herb tarts), and a tasting of several desserts round out the tea time menu. Customers get a chance to try new dishes at the teas, and popular items are added to the daily menus at later dates.

One dining room is decorated with a country-style apple motif in a green and red color scheme and natural woodwork. A second dining room is more pastel, Victorian, and has white, painted furniture. A collection of old unmatching china is their favorite dinnerware. "We know we've been busy when we're down to the white plates," said Becky.

The exterior of the building, an 1800's store and residence, will be spruced up this year with window boxes for flowers, landscaping, and Victorian moldings. Bobbi laughed about an outside door that needed painting. She said that they'd left the door to paint, not remembering you couldn't paint exterior building parts in the winter like you can in California.

When they decided to open a tea room, they decided it needed to be in a small town. "That's part of the atmosphere and makes it kind of special," said Bobbi. I heartily agree.

Finding this tea room can be a little confusing. They are located on the Iowa side of the street in a town with a Minnesota post office. Their phone has an Iowa prefix. Or, to make things very simple, you could join one of the Iowa tea room tours to this little jewel and get delivered right to Just a Bite's front door.

MARTHA'S COFFEE STATION
CHEROKEE, IOWA

A hot tip from the western part of Iowa had alerted me that Martha's Coffee Station might be of interest to manic-compulsive tea room goers such as myself (our numbers are growing daily), but I wasn't prepared for the exuberant atmosphere of the morning pick-me-up spot in downtown Cherokee, Iowa.

Atmosphere is an expected amenity in tea rooms, but Martha's owners have expanded on the concept to exceed the expected. Part of the tea room's beauty comes from the natural appointments of the old railroad depot in which it is located. Grandiose ceilings and windows provide plenty of light and a spacious feeling. The real sparkle comes from the artful use of color (mauves and greens), fabrics, wall stenciling, and the displays of gift items in the series of antique wall units that line the room. Bins of coffee beans release their appealing aromas to further enhance the ambience of this gem.

Margaret Woltman and her sister-in-law, Becky Patterson, opened Martha's in one half of the vacated Illinois Central train depot on September 8, 1993. Grant money is on the way to restore the rest of the building (on the National Historic Register) and to create a museum.

Martha's Coffee Station is the namesake of Margaret's mother, Martha Patterson. She was a very community-minded citizen of Cherokee until her passing several years ago.

A clerk at the town's lovely general store spoke highly of Martha's Coffee Station. She described the place as "very good for the community." Margaret and Becky said they've been grateful for the enthusiastic support of local residents and regular customers from surrounding towns such as Holstein, Marcus, and Aurelius. Some tea room owners report a lack of local support and rely on out-of-town diners. This is not the case in Cherokee.

Open from 8:00 until 11:30 a.m. on Monday through

Saturday, the tea room is available by reservation for afternoon group luncheons or parties. These afternoon events are sometimes daily occurrences. The ladies say they are fond of serving meals that are special and items that are unlikely to be served at home on a regular basis. Turkey lasagna has been a resounding favorite—as are the stuffed pasta and chicken breast entrees.

The morning menu is a proliferation of midwestern delicacies such as homemade cinnamon or caramel rolls and coffeecake. Healthy muffins such as the wholewheat carrot flavor have been concocted from low fat, high fiber recipes. The drink menu has been spiced up with the addition of French press and flavored coffees. A special treat at Martha's is their iced citrus drinks which include syrup flavorings such as almond and butterscotch. Four-star cheesecakes and cookies are waiting for late-morning munchers.

Cherokee is unlike most of northwestern Iowa because its terrain is a series of hills and valleys—a great place for the flatlanders to train for the celebrated annual bicycle ride across Iowa. Margaret and Becky said four-wheel driven vehicles and horses are important needs of local farmers as they tend their livestock. It's a lovely place.

But is a coffee station a tea room? I wouldn't put many of the coffee houses I see in the same category. Some coffee rooms in England are categorized by authors as tea rooms; and Martha's meets and exceeds my tea room standards for service, food, and atmosphere. I think its name was a perfect marketing ploy for a business in a small town. It's truck driver and farmer friendly—just like its cheerful hostesses!

Cherokee, Iowa

TEA FOR FIFTY

4 cups sugar
1 1/2 cups water
1 cup lemon juice
4 cups orange juice
6 cups pineapple juice
2 quarts weak tea
1-67 ounce bottle ginger ale
Fresh mint, orange, lemon, lime slices (optional)

Mix sugar and water in medium saucepan. Bring to a boil, and boil one minute. Cool mixture. Combine cooled sugar syrup, juices, and tea. Place in a punch bowl. Add ginger ale before serving, and garnish with fruit slices, mint, or decorative ice ring.

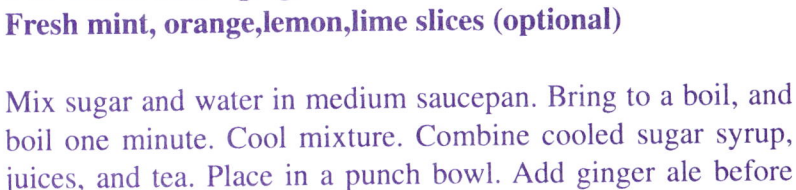

This is a favorite recipe for special parties and open houses held at Martha's Coffee Station.

ONE OF A KIND
CENTERVILLE, IOWA

"I thought he'd taken leave of his senses," said Joyce Stufflebeem. She and her husband, Jack, are the proprietors of One of a Kind—a combination bed and breakfast, tea room, and gift shop in Centerville, Iowa. She insists that the whole thing was Jack's idea. "At the time, I was doing crafts, and I think Jack thought I was overflowing our living room, and I'd have more space here." The businesses are located in a brick 1867 mansion with over thirty rooms. It's the second oldest surviving home in the town.

The Stufflebeems looked at the house for over a year before they purchased it. Many people wanted the home, but the amount of repairs that needed to be done scared them off.

After they moved in, they realized the house needed to produce income to pay for all the improvements they wanted to make. Jack thought a bed and breakfast plus a tea room would be perfect. He's a salesman—and obviously a good one—because Joyce decided to go along with the plan. Jack renovates as time allows. Things progress slowly, but Joyce is able to maintain her sense of humor—an indicator that there is hope for eventual completion of the complicated project.

According to local scuttlebutt, a doctor built the structure in 1867 to be a hospital, a tuberculosis clinic, or an insane asylum. His plans never materialized. It became his residence and later a hotel until 1928. Then a gentleman named Frank Miller bought it, and it was a boarding house and a funeral home until after World War II. Miller's son had a large family, so he kept it as his residence and continued to operate the funeral home. It sat empty for five years before the Stufflebeems purchased it in 1991.

At the time of this writing, there are five guest rooms. They are not certain how far they will expand that end of the business. This year they began advertising in several Iowan publications

Centerville, Iowa

and a Christian bed and breakfast guide book. "We have a surprising number of people go through here," said Joyce. There are four good-sized companies in town with business traffic. "A lady from California was here, and she said we really know how to keep a secret." Centerville is located about 90 miles south of Des Moines.

One of a Kind's tea room strives to cook with low fat, low calorie products as much as possible. "We seek to serve 'good for you foods' that also taste delicious." said Joyce. There are always a few exceptions. Their homemade croissants with a choice of fillings, breads, and desserts are among their most popular items. The coconut cream and chocolate French silk pies are two dessert favorites. Elegante chicken soup is popular year-round.

Collectibles, antiques, and reproduction antique furniture provide that feeling of yesteryear that is so precious to tea room lovers. The gift shop is filled with hand-crafted items, original paintings by local artists, etc.

Beautiful Lake Rathbun is only twelve minutes away with all kinds of lake activities, nature trails, and the world's largest fish hatchery. Centerville is a quiet town with several shops to entice antique hounds and an old-fashioned town square—a good rejuvenation center for frazzled nerves.

One of a Kind is a treasure trove of recreational opportunities. The quiet pace of a small town can be sheer heaven, and the tea room is a sanctuary of comforting food. Sounds like a great deal—even if it **was** all Jack's idea.

SCOTTISH EGGS

4 ounces ground sausage, raw
1/2 cup bread crumbs
1 egg
2 tablespoons minced onions, fresh
2 tablespoons fresh parsley, chopped (or 1 teaspoon dried parsley flakes)
1/4 teaspoon salt
1/8 teaspoon dried sage
1/8 teaspoon dried thyme
dash of pepper
4 hard boiled eggs, peeled

Mix all ingredients in a small bowl (except the eggs). Shape mixture around the hard boiled eggs. Bake in a covered dish for 20 minutes at 350°. Remove the cover the last 5 minutes of baking.

Serve warm with sweet mustard sauce.

SWEET MUSTARD SAUCE

2 tablespoons Dijon mustard
1 tablespoon sugar
1 1/2 tablespoons wine vinegar
1/2 teaspoon salt
1 teaspoon fresh dill (or dried dill, to taste)
1/3 cup salad oil

In a small bowl, mix all the ingredients— except the salad oil. Gradually add the oil, whipping with a fork until smooth.

Joyce serves this dish to tea room customers or bed and breakfast guests.

Centerville, Iowa

GOURMET FRENCH TOAST

1-8 ounce package light cream cheese
1 teaspoon vanilla
pinch of salt
1 teaspoon, or to taste, sugar or other sweetener
1/2 cup chopped walnuts
1 loaf French bread
4 eggs
1 cup whipping cream
1/2 teaspoon vanilla
1/2 teaspoon nutmeg, freshly ground
apricot preserves
orange juice

Beat the cream cheese, vanilla, salt, and sugar in a small bowl until smooth. Stir in the walnuts. Set aside.

Slice the French bread into slices about 1 1/2 inches thick. Cut a long, rectangular pocket out of each slice to make a place to add the cheese filling. Save the bread that is removed for later use. Fill each slice with cheese mixture. Stick a bit of the reserved bread crust in the slit to prevent the cheese from running out when cooking. Beat the eggs, whipping cream, vanilla, and nutmeg in a medium bowl. Dip the bread in the egg mixture. Slowly brown on both sides. Serve with a dollop of whipped cream or whipped topping and apricot glaze.

APRICOT GLAZE

Heat the apricot preserves in a glass measure in the microwave with enough orange juice to produce the consistency you desire. Stir to mix and prevent scorching.

THE OWL HOUSE TEA ROOM
WALNUT, IOWA

One look at the picture of the bright yellow Owl House, and I was hooting with laughter. Who would have thought it was possible to build a house with a respectable resemblance to an owl? Carol Rosenbaum, owner of the Owl House Tea Room said, "I didn't choose the name. It came with the property. It's always been called the Owl House." She said her information about the house is local folklore. The story is that the Victorian people were very superstitious. They believed that evil spirits couldn't sit on peaks because they would slide down. Therefore, in 1890 the Owl House was built with two peaks—a sort of a double insurance policy in those days.

The Owl House tea room in Walnut, Iowa, is located about 65 miles west of Des Moines on Interstate 80. More than 200 antique dealers have joined forces to form "Iowa's Antique City." The tea room is only a half block from many of the antique stores.

Originally, Carol had a gift shop in the house and rented space for the tea room to two other ladies. When they went out of business in 1990, Carol gathered her wits, mustered her confidence, and decided to try her hand in the hospitality business. She realized she'd miss the customers that had become regular guests. "I love to entertain!" she said. "I love to pamper anyone who comes for lunch or dessert."

The walls of the tea room are painted in shades of mauve, and the wooden floor is painted pink with an area rug in the center. Carol likes to change the window treatments and table coverings often. There's a small hall leading to the tea room where, as time permits, she is completing a pond scene mural with cat tails, rocks, trees, flowers, and lily pads.

Carol delights in finding unusual service dishes. She's found salt and pepper shakers that look like daisies and favors unusual dessert plates. Tea-drinking customers are treated by the use of

Walnut, Iowa

whimsical owl teapots made of a lusterware china. She sells the teapots in her gift shop and says she tries to find owl gift items as some customers come in specifically looking for them.

Morning coffee delicacies at the Owl House include eye-opening, homemade pecan rolls, muffins, and monkey bread. Lunches include such things as quiche, soups, sandwiches (such as the chicken cashew pita), and special homemade entrees. Carol's chicken casserole and beef stroganoff have been two favorites. There's turtle cheesecake and chocolate mousse, but the stars of the desert line-up are the apple dumplings with homemade cinnamon sauce. The tea room is well known for these dumplings.

Carol loves owning her tea room. She says it's the perfect mate for her gift shop. After four years she has not lost her zest for entertaining. "It's such a positive thing," she said. "People are in town spending their money and having a great time. I try to make things nice for them and to make them welcome." She's a very wise woman—every pun intended.

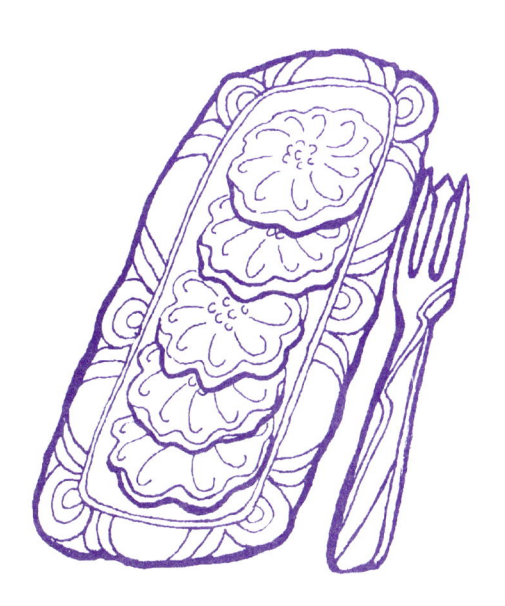

PINA COLADA MUFFINS

1 egg
2 cups variety baking mix
1/2 cup crushed pineapple, drained
1/2 cup shredded coconut
2 tablespoons sugar
2/3 cup orange juice

Mix all the above ingredients in a medium bowl. Pour into twelve lightly greased muffin cups. Bake at 375° for 15 minutes or until lightly browned. Glaze while still warm.

Glaze:
3/4 cup powdered sugar
1/2 teaspoon rum extract
2-3 teaspoons milk

Mix the above ingredients together in a small bowl. Spread on the warm muffins.

This recipe was given to Carol by a customer. "It's a very big hit with my morning coffee customers."

TEA THYME AT SADIE'S
FORT DODGE, IOWA

Tea Thyme at Sadie's is a dream-come-true in a real sense for owner, Deb Lacina. It started when she woke up one night from a dream. In her dream, she owned a tea room in a vintage house with old-fashioned chairs. She didn't want to forget this one—she got out of bed and started scribbling notes.

Deb decided to act on her dream, but she was unable to find a suitable old house for her tea room. She did find an old plumbing shop which was attached to Sister Sadie's of Iowa gift shop in a good location only one block south of Highway 20 in Fort Dodge. Sister Sadie's specializes in floral designs, jewelry, collectibles, linens, and all the other staples a devout tea room lover needs. The gift shop and tea room complement each other perfectly.

Tea Thyme at Sadie's is a large dining room with lace-covered tables and old-fashioned pressed-back chairs. The ceiling is high and vaulted. Deb selected a floral carpeting and took a piece of wallpaper she thought would be suitable to a friend who was a decorator for a second opinion. Her friend picked up a wallpaper sample book which almost fell open to a floral wallpaper that was an uncanny match to Deb's carpeting. It was a perfect choice and another step to the fulfillment of the tea room dream. Although opening her tea room was not without stressful times, Deb says many aspects fell as easily into place as that wallpaper book fell open. She feels her tea room was meant to happen.

Deb had previously been a long-term employee of a hotel chain. She'd done waitressing, supervising, and catering sales. She was also the winner of the coveted car award as a successful cosmetics consultant. Her experience has made her one of the few tea room owners I've talked with who had a background in the hospitality field and a realistic picture of what it would take to operate her own place. She certainly has grasped a very accurate picture of the tea room concept. "We try to make every lunch a special occasion," she said.

Sadie's menu is small but inspired. Some of its features are a creamed soup in a bread bowl and Sadie's Salad (with grilled chicken breast, lettuce, artichoke hearts, and homemade raspberry vinaigrette dressing). Deb's coconut cream pie receives rave reviews because its coconut crust accentuates its goodness. Teas, coffees, cappuccinos, and French press coffees are highlights of the beverage menu. Deb and her staff enjoy developing their own recipes for the tea room's rotating menu.

Tea Thyme at Sadie's is supported by a luncheon crowd that is a good mixture of men and women. Deb serves many special Sunday brunches and is happy to accommodate private parties. Her zest for her work is evident as she makes the rounds to her customers' tables to greet them and exchange pleasantries.

I didn't dream about visiting Tea Thyme at Sadie's, but I did listen to the small voice within me that urged me to find the tea room. I was greeted at the door by a face from my past. Gail Casey and I had been employed by a food service management company in Cedar Rapids, Iowa, and we'd both left the area about two years ago. I was surprised to hear she was living in Fort Dodge with her new husband, and she was surprised to find me writing a book about tea rooms.

Fort Dodge is the largest Iowa town close to the northwest section of the state and is quite well known as a retail hub. Shoppers from as far away as Des Moines and Ankeny are lured to its specialty shops in the newly renovated downtown. Its residents and visitors are now part of the formerly tea room-deprived sector of the midwestern population—thanks to dreaming Deb Lacina and her dream-come-true, Tea Thyme at Sadie's.

Fort Dodge, Iowa

FRENCH TACOS

2 pounds ground beef, cooked, drained and crumbled
1-1.25 ounces package taco seasoning mix
1/2 cup sour cream
1/2 cup shredded cheddar cheese
8 puff pastry squares, thawed

In a small bowl, mix the beef, seasoning, sour cream, and shredded cheese. Place 4 ounces of the meat mixture in the center of a puff pastry square. Pull the four corners of the pastry square together in the center (like a diaper), and tuck closed with a toothpick. Bake at 375°-400° until golden brown (20-30 minutes). Remove the toothpick. Place on a plate garnished with black olives slices, chopped green onion, chopped tomatoes, shredded cheese, salsa, and sour cream.

Purchased or homemade con queso sauce makes a good topping.

This dish has a nice presentation and is often served with Spanish rice at Tea Thyme at Sadie's.

CON QUESO SAUCE

1 pound American cheese loaf
4 ounces picante sauce

Melt the cheese in the microwave, stirring often to prevent scorching. Stir in the picante sauce.

THYMES REMEMBERED
PERRY, IOWA

I'd been curious about this Perry tea room for a long time and was determined to discover how Thymes Remembered has gained the status of being one of the premier tea rooms in Iowa. The exterior of the building provided no clues, although I noticed the sprawling, brick cottage sat positioned in a strategic intersection of Highway 144 and is just six blocks north of Highway 141. It's only about 25 miles to the state's capitol city from Perry. A large, free-standing sign provided a hint of the spirit of hospitality inside—"Because We All Love to Share a Special Time" was the heartfelt motto.

Things became more clear as I, ready for serious investigation, strolled into the Calico Shoppes that Ramona Birdsell has presided over for 15 years. The shops were a series of many rooms of quality gifts in every variety. I couldn't think of a single gift that was missing.

A friendly lady directed me to the tea room addition at the back of the building, and suddenly it all became more obvious. The look of the tea room was ethereal: a soaring, vaulted ceiling and a central arched window of grandiose proportions, tall pressed-back, antique chairs, statuesque crystal vases with profuse silk and natural floral arrangements. I'd never noticed a tea room before where the central decorating theme was "tall." My lofty expectations of Thymes Remembered were fulfilled. It was lovely.

A huge Christmas tree, decorated for the season with a bounty of pastel flowers, flanked an old oak fireplace front which was decked with bunnies. Floral wallpaper border rimmed the vaulted ceiling lines. As perfect as her tea room is, Ramona is not content to leave things status quo. She'd recently replaced her china with a fresh garden pattern and said she'd ordered cranberry-glass light fixtures to replace those in the dining room. The waitresses donned fresh, floral, spring-like jumpers. One of them

Perry, Iowa

told me their outfits change with the seasons. Perhaps Ramona's habit of constantly upgrading amenities and responding to new trends is one of her secrets of tea room fame.

Besides being a successful decorator, she is also an excellent hostess. During our lunch together, many customers stopped by to tell her goodbye and to tell her they'd had a nice time in the tea room. She excused herself several times to greet customers or chat a moment at their tables. The guests thoroughly enjoyed the recognition and attention she bestowed upon them.

She gave me a guided tour through lunch—teaching the rudiments of French press coffee brewing, sharing experiences to give me a better understanding of the tea room than I could get by merely observing. Thymes Remembered serves three to five entree selections and ten to fifteen desserts each day. It's all homemade, irresistible, and in profound proportions. Her husband and partner, Jim, insists on good value; therefore, you can expect larger servings than in many tea rooms. Because so many people are celebrating special events by dining at Thymes Remembered, they don't seem to mind; and the waitress reported most customers indulge in dessert. Ramona told me that she sees the low fat dieting trend expanding to tea room fare and is planning adjustments to the menu for serious dieters.

The kitchen staff devotes time to food presentation techniques. My chicken Florentine with cold fruit soup and tea breads plate was garnished with a leaf of pastel colored kale on which pineapple and spiced apple rings lay entwined. The garnish was completed by a fresh carnation. Ramona said they use fresh flowers on the plate several times per week. Other special table accoutrements were crystal knife rests at each place setting and crystal salt and pepper shakers shaped like grape clusters hanging from silver trees.

The French press coffee was served with a comprehensive condiment platter including souffle cups of milk chocolate pieces, cream mint candies, whipped cream, a cinnamon stick, and a pirouette stick cookie. Coffee grounds are allowed to steep a few minutes in the glass pot. Then a plunger is manually depressed to push the grounds to the bottom of the pot, and the brewed coffee is poured off—producing the freshest cup of coffee possible.

Entree selections on the day I visited were chicken Florentine with cold fruit soup and crunchy almond chicken with salad. Seafood lovers were tempted by seafood supreme with salad. At dessert time, I was faced with the awful job of selecting from bread pudding smothered with hot rum sauce, apple pie and ice cream dripping with caramel sauce, weighty cheesecakes, aristocratic Italian creme cake, and rice pudding dressed with raspberry sauce. The apple pie with fixings rivaled the quality of my mother's recipe. (Sorry, Mom!)

Ramona modestly declined my labeling her tea room as a legend when I questioned her about the tea room's fame; but the lady in the floral department was not shy. "Because it's the best!" was her simple answer. She also said that people come there because of Ramona and the staff's royal treatment of their guests.

I pieced my findings together to form a conclusion about Thymes Remembered's recipe for success. It's a long list: congenial treatment by hostess and staff, attention to decorating details, high standards of food quality, visible location near a major city but with a small town atmosphere, constant changes to keep the look fresh, and an extensive gift shop. I concluded that Ramona could write a guide to tea room success. Even Hollywood couldn't create a more perfect tea room than she has. Thymes Remembered richly deserves the honorable reputation that has been heaped upon it.

CHICKEN BROCCOLI CASSEROLE

1-6 ounce package long grain and wild rice mix, cooked
1-16 ounce package frozen chopped broccoli, thawed
3 cups cooked, diced chicken
1 cup American processed cheese, shredded
1 cup fresh, sliced mushrooms
1/2 cup mayonnaise
1-10 3/4 ounce can cream of mushroom soup
1/4 teaspoon dry mustard
1/4 teaspoon curry powder
1/4 cup parmesan cheese (or to taste)
1/2 cup crushed croutons or cracker crumbs
1 tablespoon butter

Preheat oven to 350°. In a lightly greased or sprayed 9" by 13" pan, layer rice, broccoli, chicken, cheese, and mushrooms. In a small bowl, combine mayonnaise, soup, mustard, and curry powder. Pour over the chicken mixture. Sprinkle with parmesan cheese. Saute croutons or cracker crumbs in butter, and sprinkle over the cheese. Bake for 30 minutes or until bubbling hot.

Serves 6.

WISCONSIN

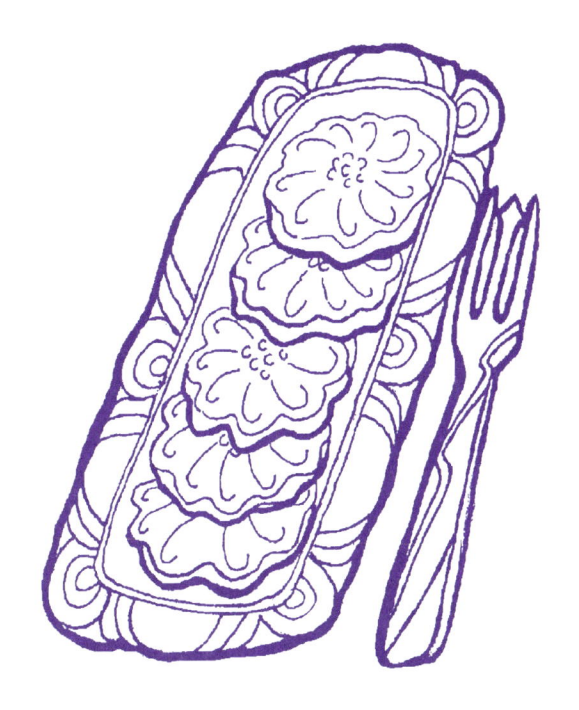

Wisconsin

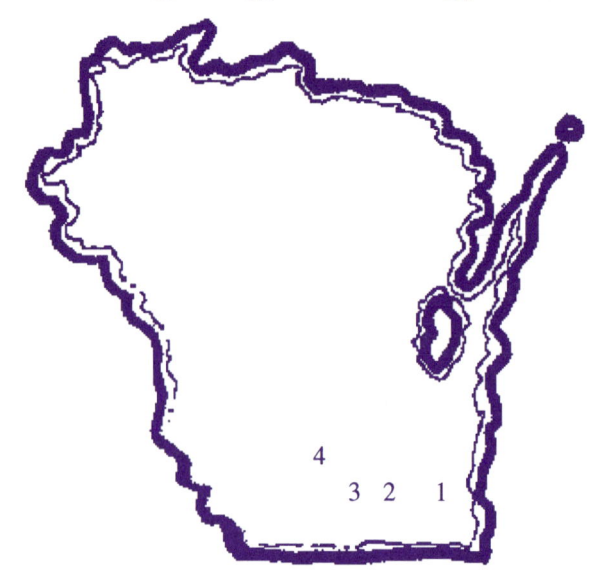

1. Bit's of Britain, Milwaukee
2. Bit's of Britain, Waukesha
3. Queen Belle Boutique & Tea Room, Oconomowoc
4. New Glarus Bakery and Tea Room, New Glarus

BITS OF BRITAIN TEA ROOM
MILWAUKEE, WISCONSIN

Don't breeze into Bits of Britain with hopes of discovering a feminine, Victorian place or a tea room resembling those in European hotels. You'll find Bits of Britain to be an unpretentious tea room such as those found in neighborhoods outside London's boundaries. If the tea room's authentic atmosphere rubs off on you, you might catch yourself gaily traipsing out singing its praises with a newfound, clipped accent.

June Gray and Diana Edwardsen, a lively mother-daughter combo, welcome guests to their Bay View tea room near the Port of Milwaukee. June is all I envision an English woman to be: polite, dignified, outspoken, with an arid sense of humor. Though American and more casual than her mother, Diana shares her quick wit. The tea room has a 20 year history, and the ladies have owned it for nine years. Neither had any experience in the food service business. Diane laughs when she says she thought it was going to be a nice part-time job to balance her status as a young mother. June, a 20 year insurance veteran, said purchasing the tea room was like jumping into the deep end of a swimming pool with no life-support or knowledge of swimming. "There's no room here for a hostess," she said. "The hostess also washes dishes, bakes, or does whatever else is needed."

Diana says little of their sales come from "walk-in" business. Guests drive to the tea room from all over the city, Midwest, and United States. Word of mouth advertising has been the key; but the tea room has been featured in many city newspapers, an eating guide to Milwaukee, and on television.

Although I'm taking the risk of sounding like a real estate advertisement, I must label this tea room "charming." It was formerly a neighborhood grocery store, and much of that character has been retained. Its frontage remains a general store. The old, working ice box with original meat hooks stands behind a wood and glass counter. Margaret Thatcher's photograph greets guests from its vantage point high on the wall. The tea room, kitchen, and "W.C." occupy the former grocer's quarters in the back of the building.

Tables set with mismatched English china are ready for diners who will enjoy home-cooked English cuisine, one of nine afternoon tea variations, or dessert from their large repertoire of sweets.

Piping hot, delectable, meat pies are the backbone of the luncheon "Bill of Fare" menu: steak, steak and kidney, chicken, cheese, pork, Scottish meat pies and Cornish pasties. All are served with Branston pickles (a tart, brown relish), English cheese, and mushy peas. June explained the bright green mushy peas are made from dried peas cooked to the consistency of a super-thick pea soup and sightly sweetened and served with a cruet of malt vinegar. They were developed as a source of protein in days when meat sources were rare. Even my formerly vegetable-hating husband thought they were tasty. The steak pie with mushrooms and onions was excellent. The steak was tender, gravy was flavorful; and the crust was perfectly browned and flaky.

A compendium of desserts features items from the British Isles. I was thrilled to try Devon cream on a homemade scone. I'd been under the impression it couldn't be purchased in the United States. It's extremely thick and buttery and is made from the cream of English Jersey cows. June gave me her version of the answer to the tea room riddle: which goes on the scone first—the cream or the preserves? She said she prefers the cream as the ultimate scone topping but admitted it's a regional preference.

Ten flavors of shortbread (butter) biscuits, scones, lemon curd tarts, hazelnut bars, Queen Victoria sponge, Eccles cake, and other desserts are available daily. Other desserts named for members of the Royal Family (such as the Fergie) are also featured. June describes the decadent display as "labor intensive." Special desserts are also prepared. Our waitress urged us to try the orange chocolate cream Victoria sponge cake. It was flavored with triple sec and

Milwaukee, Wisconsin

frosted with a smooth, peachy-colored frosting. The ample wedge was edged with a row of silver, candy beads and accented with a showy triangle of candied orange. Rich Snowdon pudding with fluffy white sauce is like a Hostess cupcake that grew up. That's how Diana described one of the most popular Bits of Britain desserts. The very adult, steamed, fudge cupcake was a new sensation for my desert-loving tastebuds.

Traditional libations at the tea room included teas, coffee, Cadbury drinking chocolate, milk, and soda.

Afternoon tea at the Bits of Britain may be traditional high tea with tea sandwiches, Scottish salmon, fresh fruit, and tea. The gentleman's tea comes with a freshly baked pork pie (served cold), mushy peas, Branston pickle relish, cheese, and tea. A Welsh tea includes the yummy Snowdon pudding, choice of tart, and tea. Other adult teas include: classic cream, Scottish, and Bits of Britain lady's tea. Junior teas (the Prince Harry and Prince William teas) provide a treat to suit the taste of youngsters.

Before you leave Bits of Britain, take a gander at the plethora of products from the British Isles. There are tins, china, bath products, books and flossies (glossy British magazines). Most of the tea room's desserts, teas, English cheeses, and entrees are available to take home. You may also purchase Devon cream, marmalades, or Branston pickles. The ladies sell their own scone mixes so you can practice being "veddy British" at home. I made the best batch of scones I've ever made using their golden raisin mix.

Bay View is an interesting ethnic pocket in Milwaukee. It's located on Lake Michigan near the Yacht Club, Coast Guard station, Marine and Naval Reserve units. June explained that a steel mill was built there many years ago when labor was in short supply. Workers were imported from mills in Sheffield, England. The old row houses in Bay View are reminiscent of Sheffield homes. The neighborhood had later influxes from Italian and Polish immigrants.

Bits of Britain Tea Room

It would be to your best welfare to race to Bits of Britain if you are interested in expanding your knowledge about tea rooms. As my husband astutely observed: "Bits of Britain is as British as you can get within the confines of the United States." The day after our visit, we were already lamenting about not purchasing enough goodies to last until our next trip to Milwaukee.

If you hear any nasty rumors about the mediocre cuisine of the British, plug your ears; and refer the blasphemous gossiper to Bits of Britain for a proper adjustment of attitude.

Milwaukee, Wisconsin

QUEEN MOTHER'S CAKE

2 tablespoons fine, dry bread crumbs
1 1/2 cups slivered almonds (6 ounces),
	ground to a fine powder
6 ounces semi-sweet chocolate chips
3/4 cup unsalted butter, softened
3/4 cup sugar
6 eggs, separated
1/8 teaspoon salt

Preheat oven to 375°. Butter a 9-inch springform pan. Line bottom with waxed paper. Butter paper, and dust with breadcrumbs. Melt chocolate chips in a double boiler or in the microwave. Set aside. In small mixing bowl, cream the butter. Add sugar and beat at medium high speed until dissolved (about 2 minutes). Add egg yolks, one at a time, beating well after each addition. Add the melted chocolate, and beat on low speed until just mixed, scraping sides of bowl often. Add almonds, and stir until just mixed. Transfer mixture to a large bowl, and set aside.

In a second large mixing bowl, beat the egg whites (using clean beaters) until soft peaks form. Stir 1 cup of the egg whites into chocolate mixture with a rubber spatula. Fold in the remaining egg whites in 2 additions. Bake for 20 minutes at 375°. Reduce heat to 350°, and bake 50 minutes longer. Don't overbake. Cake will be soft and moist in the center. Cool on a wet towel for 20 minutes, remove from pan. Remove the pan bottom and waxed paper. Cool on rack, right side up. Trim cake with serrated knife so top is flat when cool.

Bits of Britain also treats lovers of Anglo food in its new Waukesha, Wisconsin tea room.

FROSTING FOR QUEEN MOTHER'S CAKE

**1/2 cup heavy cream
2 teaspoons dry, instant coffee
8 ounces semi-sweet chocolate chips**

In a heavy pan, scald cream over medium heat until bubbles form around the edge. Whisk in coffee until dissolved. Add chocolate chips and heat, stirring occasionally for 1 minute; and remove from heat. Continue to stir until chocolate is melted and mixture is smooth.

Let frosting cool, stirring occasionally. When cool, gently mix, and pour it over top of the cake, allowing to drizzle down the sides of the cake. Smooth frosting on the top and sides with spatula.

BANOFFI PIE

**1/2 cup butter
9 ounces gingersnap cookies, crushed
1/2 cup white sugar
3/4 cup butter
1-14 ounce can sweetened, condensed milk
2 bananas, sliced and dipped in lemon juice
1 cup heavy cream, whipped to soft peaks
1 ounce shaved chocolate**

Melt the 1/2 cup butter, and stir in the gingersnap crumbs. Press into the bottom and sides of a 7 1/2-inch flan pan with a loose bottom, and chill. In a non-stick saucepan, melt the 3/4 cup butter; add sugar and milk. Stirring constantly, bring to a low boil and simmer for exactly 5 minutes to make a light, golden caramel. Pour over crust and cool. Top with whipped cream, bananas, and chocolate.

NEW GLARUS BAKERY AND TEA ROOM
NEW GLARUS, WISCONSIN

"If I'm going to run a restaurant, I want to be able to eat there," said weight-watching tea room owner, Nancy Weber. On the drive to New Glarus, I'd been thinking how fortunate I am to live just a few blocks from a liposuction center; but I felt even more blessed when Nancy talked to me about her thoughts on nutritious tea room food.

"People come here for lighter food," said Nancy. "Swiss food is typically fried or in heavy sauces. Everyone who visits our Swiss settlement should have one of these meals. But people can't eat like that all the time, and that's why they come to us."

New Glarus, America's Little Switzerland, was settled in 1845 by immigrants from Glarus, Switzerland, who dreamed of better economic futures. Glarus is located in the Germanic section of Switzerland. Nancy and Howard, a baker who trained in Lucerne, Switzerland, first heard about New Glarus on an Icelandic flight home from the old country. A lady on the plane mentioned the Swiss settlement. Sixteen years ago the Webers were visiting a friend in Madison who mentioned the Swiss bakery in New Glarus. They took a short drive to New Glarus, and there was the bakery that had operated since 1915—for sale. Howard had been working in restaurants, and this was his chance to use all his Swiss training.

Eight years ago, they decided to make use of the upstairs space for their European tea room. In Switzerland, there are many bakery and tea room combinations where the breads are produced by the bakeries and the tea room handle the dessert production. The former apartment was gutted, and the Webers patterned their tea room after what they'd seen in Europe. It's light and airy with large, lace-curtained windows. Oak shelves top the windows and decorate the walls. They hold antique baking artifacts such as cookie and candy molds, and a collection of statues of bakers. The overall look is casual, crisp, and unfussy.

Nancy explained that the authenticity of European cuisine sometimes must be compromised to better suit American tastes. Authentic Swiss pastries are typically a little more dry, while Americans prefer moister, sweeter, more fresh desserts and breads. The Europeans use unsalted butter, unsweetened whipping cream, and hazelnuts are the most popular nut. Americans generally use shortening, sweetened whipped cream, and almonds or pecans.

Salads such as the strawberry spinach and special chicken salads are very popular in the tea room, but Nancy says the real menu stars are the sandwiches. I was having a hard time deciding what to order (as usual), and I asked Nancy to make a recommendation. She and the chef decided the chicken herb burger would be a representative choice of their cuisine. It was a savory sensation made of chicken bits and fresh garden herbs that were pressed together, grilled and served on a crusty wheat roll with a flavored mustard on the side. Three painfully delicious side salads that are immortalized in my memory accompanied my burger. All were low fat, highly spiced, and very colorful. They included tabbouleh (made with cracked wheat, green onions, and many spices), a shredded carrot salad, and a cranberry orange relish.

I needed no assistance whatsoever when it came to selecting my dessert (funny how that works). The bakery and tea room is sort of like a theme park for dessert lovers. There's something for everyone, and the hazelnut praline torte looked like my ride to dessert bliss. Howard is partial to lighter desserts. Therefore, the torte was a nice, airy sponge with thin layers of German-style buttercream (made with real butter, not shortening). The small wedge was topped with a tiny dollop of whipped cream and a single, perfect hazelnut. Other marvelous looking creations included raspberry apple strudel, a chocolate torte with fresh raspberry filling and creamy ganache, apricot torte with a refreshing apricot mousse, apple flan (European equivalent of apple pie), and a white chocolate Swiss rouladen. Two pies are offered each day—another American preference. Nancy says the elderberry apple is an extremely popular choice.

Drinks are an important part of the tea room's menu because many people come in to have coffee and the bakery's famous hard rolls or pastries for breakfast or afternoon tea. Iced and hot teas are prepared with loose teas which are Nancy's preference because she feels they are more flavorful. Herbal teas are available in tea bags. Victor Allen gourmet coffee beans are used for their other coffee creations. The cafe latte is their most popular coffee—a European style coffee mixed with frothy milk. The chocolate cappuccino is half espresso and half hot chocolate, and the plain cappuccino is espresso topped with mounds of frothed milk. There's a zero calorie espresso made with rich, French roast beans.

Only the best quality ingredients are used in the tea room and bakery. Howard's gardens provide ample supplies of currants, gooseberries, raspberries, and strawberries. He also gleans the fresh herbs for many dishes and the flowers for the tables from his beloved garden.

Nancy is carefully adjusting the tea room's menu and recipes to reflect the low fat dining trend. Her degree in dietetics and her sense of personal consciousness makes this a priority. "I like to think I have something to offer the diabetic customers that come in," she said. The vision is also applied to the bakery end of the business, but it is much harder to produce desserts that are low in fat and sugar that will retain customer acceptability. However, many of their crusty, hearth-baked breads are naturally low in fat and all other nasty enemies of the dieter.

The bakery, and all that is in it, has a warm, European style. The selection was quite a change from American bakery fare—whole loaves of breads and a full array of European pastries: linzer, Swedish tarts, springerle, fruit-filled cookie pockets, bratzeli, torte, flan, etc. Currant scones were called "fat rascals."

New Glarus Bakery and Tea Room

It was a crowded place. The heat index was 105° outside, and I first thought people were just coming in to the air conditioning to re-solidify. I watched the pedestrian traffic around town, and I realized they were all congregating in the bakery. It was busy for hours. As I stood in line to make my purchases, I heard a man whisper to his wife in a reverent tone, "Look at it! It's just like in Europe."

New Glarus is located in the Uplands region of southwestern Wisconsin and is just south of Madison in the rolling hills of Green County. It's a village of many ethnic festivals such as the Heidi Festival, Wilhelm Tell Festival, Volkfest (Swiss Independence Day), etc. There's a plethora of Swiss museums, a Swiss lace factory, the Sugar River Bike Trail, many shops, and restaurants. Nancy said many people visit New Glarus to purchase cheese and sausages, and much of her business is from repeat out-of-towners.

The week before I made my pilgrimage to this precious town, I was talking to a man about my project and told him I was planning a trip to New Glarus. He'd been there a few years ago on a rainy, spring day, with his family, and he couldn't say enough good about the time they had in the little tea room over the bakery. He described it as "so European, so authentic, and so honest," and said it sounded kind of funny; but it was the highlight of their trip. It didn't sound so funny to me. Every time I go to a tea room, I see families and friends relishing the time they spend with each other—pouring over picture albums, re-living the old days, and sharing lots of laughter. It does my heart good.

New Glarus, Wisconsin

SHRIMP POTATO AND PEA SALAD

2 1/2 pounds small cooked shrimp, shelled
10 red or wax-skin potatoes, cooked, peeled, and diced
1 pound plus 9 ounces frozen peas, thawed, blanched, drained, and cooled
8 dill pickles, chopped
10 green onions, chopped
2 1/2 cups mayonnaise
1/2 cup lemon juice
2 1/2 tablespoons fresh dill weed, minced (or 2 1/2 teaspoons dried dillweed)
1 teaspoon salt
1/2 teaspoon pepper, freshly ground

In a large bowl, combine shrimp, potatoes, peas, pickles, and onions. Cover and refrigerate while preparing dressing. In a small bowl, mix together the mayonnaise, lemon juice, dillweed, salt, and pepper. Add to salad ingredients, and mix thoroughly. Refrigerate several hours or overnight. At serving time, adjust seasoning if desired. Makes approximately 15 servings.

Garnish this salad with dill pickles and pimento stuffed olives.

THE VICTORIAN BELLE TEA ROOM
OCONOMOWOC, WISCONSIN

"Come my dear. Let's go out on the veranda and talk about how beautiful our children will be." The name "Victorian Belle" conjures up all sorts of idyllic notions of mint julep afternoons. One word can adequately describe all of the enchanting businesses that Barb Jaeger has created, and that is "romantic." Her advertising invites customers to "surround yourself with the romance of the Victorian Era with timeless gifts and cherished keepsakes for those not content with the ordinary...Where dreams come true...Relax and enjoy lunch in our tea room." The lady has a way with words.

First, she opened a beautiful Victorian bed and breakfast which is just down the street from the Old Theater Mall that houses her other shops. The gift shop came second and was followed by her bridal shop. (A second gift shop is located in Sturgeon Bay, Wisconsin, which is in Door County—a vacationer's delight.) The boutique and tea room is the fourth addition to the lovely Victorian Belle continuum. When the old Russian tea room vacated the front of the building, Barb knew it would be a good place for a Victorian tea room. "Most women like to go to lunch in a small, intimate place, and that wasn't available here," she said.

The tea room is a very labor-intensive business, but Barb feels that it blends very well with her other businesses; and they all complement each other.

Barb is obviously a master buyer and a proficient display marketer. Her shops have a unique flair that seems to flow from the gifts to the clothing and bridal accoutrements. I have never seen such a collection. Judy Harris (artist of this book) was with me that day. I would think she's seen it all as she's lived in Chicago and urban California areas her entire life and is a supplier of handmade Victorian and theme jewelry to many gift shops; but she was as equally impressed. Barb says she works on her own,

Oconomowoc, Wisconsin

rarely visiting other shops, and explained, "I just go with my own ideas. Of course, I do look through *Victoria* magazine." I am a firm believer that no one should attempt to copy the work of people as talented as Barb. They will surely fail if they try to duplicate such a God-given talent.

The tea room is small, cozy, and very busy. The smell of coffee beans in lucite bins imparts a wondrous fragrance. A constantly changing menu of salad, soup, and sandwich combinations are the noon-time fare. Many people that work in the area stop for lunches-to-go (take-away as they call it in England). A beautiful, oak, refrigerated cabinet holds a good assortment of irresistible cheesecakes. Many of the lunches are served with warmed croissants and honey which makes a good marriage of flavors and textures. Muffins and bagels and other sweets are available for breakfast, brunch, or snacks. The decaffeinated apricot iced tea was especially satisfying on the warm summer's day. During our stay in England, Doug and I offered to make some iced tea for our guest house hostess who swore she had never tried it. She claimed it sounded very distasteful and had no interest in trying it. Those English folks should loosen up a bit and give iced tea a chance. It's one of those things that is sheer heaven on a beastly hot summer's day. (It must be much cooler there.)

The tea room has remnants of the appearance of its former coffee shop pedigree; but Barb has taken careful pains to soften the bistro look with mauve damask fabrics, laces, a Victorian screen, and pictures. She is gradually incorporating Victorian touches to her popular tea room. One of the best views in the house is of the ladies' boutique in the front of the store which is a Shangri-la of vestments that will even tempt non-shoppers such as myself.

Before the Victorian times, two Indian trails crossed at the four corners that are now the center of the town (the intersections of Highways 16 and 67).

The Victorian Belle Tea Room

During the latter part of the 19th century, Oconomowoc became a popular summer retreat for the Midwest's upper-crust. The names such as Anheuser, Armour, and Pabst are known to most Americans. Of course, many middleclass midwesterners joined the fringes of the Lake Country settlement.

Barb says that an aerial view of the city looks like an island. Nestled on the banks of Lac La Belle and Fowler Lakes, the Oconomowoc area is known for its many lakes and picturesque beauty. A waterfall (there's that romance thing again) separates the two lakes, and there is a proliferation of other lakes nearby.

Finally, this farm girl's question has been answered. On Friday nights, there is a stream of cars flowing northward and out of the Chicago horizon. I often wondered, "Where are they going?" Now I just ask, "May I go too?" I may be wearing my rose-colored glasses again, but it's hard to deny the sense that all my heart's desires will be met in a romantic place the Indians called "the place where the river falls."

TEAPHERNALIA

INTERNATIONAL TEA SOURCE
LONG GROVE, ILLINOIS

Just under the attic of a historic Victorian house in Long Grove, Illinois, is perched the International Tea Source, a tea shop on the cutting-edge of all that is new and exciting in the world of tea.

John Mendez, an ex-jewelry designer, is the tea master of this tea lover's heaven with over 200 kinds of teas to choose from. "We go for the unusual," he said. If Japan Genmaicha green tea with popcorn pieces and rice with the brown hulls intact isn't unusual, then I don't know what is—unless it's the variety of white teas John hopes to add to his collection.

International Tea Source has a complete selection of teaphernalia in a sprawling price range. Tea kettles sell for about $12 to $200. China and pottery items are also available in all prices, and there's a spread of food items to handle every taste. Delicacies such as whiskey flavored marmalade, flavored honeys and sugars, biscuits, shorties, and scone mixes are a few of the angelic indulgences one might find to stock one's tea time pantry. International Tea Source is also a prime source for novelty jewelry with tea themes and tea books, which I swear John has memorized from cover to cover.

Teas are available four ways: in three ounce bags of loose tea, in sacks of 25 tea bags, by the ounce from a wall of lucite bins, or by the brewed cup to sip as your peruse the rest of the tea gallery. The custom-designed bags used to package the teas are so striking that it's a shame to tuck them away in your cupboards.

I attended a tea tasting at the International Tea Source recently. It was held in the evening, by reservation, and was most enjoyable. John and his staff love tea and to talk tea with customers. The menu for the evening included cucumber sandwich triangles with dill and cream cheese spread topped with zest of lemon. The second sandwich was a Dijon egg salad with fresh herb leaves. Blueberry and plain scones, sprinkled with lemon sugar, were accompanied by a zingy lemon curd; and the desserts were samples of products featured in the shop such as Lady Walton chocolate-filled cookies and apricot or raspberry shorties (bite-sized, cinnamon-topped, short bread cakes). Iced raspberry tea was a good accompaniment for our food because hot teas were included in the tea tasting program.

We were pleased to taste and examine the leaves of three kinds of tea during the tasting: China Black (a black tea), Black Dragon Oolong (a green tea), and Pinhead Dragon Gunpowder (a golden tea). All were served in clear glass cups so that we could examine the teas as well as taste them. Next, we were given a tea list, and each guest was invited to select any tea that struck his or her fancy. I noticed the subtle differences in color, smoothness, and flavor among the teas, but I'll admit I liked them all. I believe that was because careful attention was given to the brewing processes so that no over-extraction took place to create bitterness. It's so easy to over-brew tea at home or to receive bitter tea in a restaurant. John and his staff always brew at the lower end of the brewing time table—about two minutes per cup or four minutes per pot.

One of the best features of International Tea Source is that you don't have to live within driving distance of the store to enjoy their products. You can join their tea of the month club which means you receive three kinds of tea selected for members each month and their latest newsletter which includes a survey to rate your tea preferences. The newsletter also includes recipes, tea facts and descriptions, notice of special sales, and new products in the store. A mail order catalog is near completion at the time of this writing.

You may be curious about the 200-plus tea varieties. They are priced reasonably—from $.99 per ounce to over $5.00 per ounce. If you've never purchased teas by the ounce, these prices may sound steep; but keep in mind that a pound of tea leaves is a bunch of tea, and cost per brewed cup is minimal. You can expect ten to twelve cups of tea per ounce or even double that if you prefer weak tea. The categories include: Teas of the World, Special teas, Great Rare Un-blended Estate Grown Teas, Fruit Flavors, Nuts and Spices and Other Flavors, Herbal, and Decaffeinated. Tea sources are exotic places such as the Middle East, Asia, and South America.

John's dreams are to have sit-down space in his shop so that he can serve customers a more complete service in a leisurely fashion and to franchise his stores. He and his business partner will be traveling to Austria in the fall to an international coffee and tea symposium. I'm sure he'll collect a few more dreams there.

In the summer of 1995, International Tea Source opened its second store at 3324 North Halsted in Chicago.

HOT WEATHER PUNCH

8 tea bags or 1 ounce loose tea
 (Fruit flavored teas would be a good choice.)
3 quarts boiling water
1-12 ounce can frozen lemonade concentrate
3/4 cup sugar (or to taste)
1 liter ginger ale, chilled (optional)

Steep tea bags or loose tea in the boiling water for ten minutes. Mix the prepared tea with the lemonade concentrate and sugar. Just before serving, add the ginger ale. Serve over ice.

Serves 12-15.

This tea punch would be worthy of a paper parasol and fruit garnish and makes an inexpensive drink for summer teas and parties.

FRANNIE NORTON, VICTORIAN TEA CONSULTANT
WHEATON, ILLINOIS

Frannie Norton is proof-positive that I'm not totally off my tea-sipping rocker. It's not just my imagination that the rate of old-fashioned tea taking in the Midwest is accelerating at a rate certain to exceed the speed limit of modern progress. This lady has made a career for herself as a Victorian tea consultant and historian.

Growing up in a Lithuanian neighborhood in Chicago, Frannie admitted, was not a time filled with fancy tea parties. Those tea parties were reserved for the upper class and the upper-middle echelon of society. Her European grandmother preferred to follow old customs 100 per cent of the time. "She treated you as though you were the only person in the entire house. That's the way Victorians were. They made you feel as though you were the most important person in life," said Frannie. Her grandmother served Frannie and her sisters honey tea with yellow, raisin bread for a special treat. "Aunt Sophie always used special tablecloths and dishes; and Aunt Jane's house was like having tea all the time," she said. But in those days, in her ethnic community, it was never called tea. "It never had a name," she said.

While working as a volunteer for the DuPage County Historical Museum, Frannie was asked to make an authentic Victorian floral arrangement. She had formerly studied the art of floral design but needed to do research before tackling this assignment. She quickly fell into a time warp that has not ceased to hold her attention. The history of Victorian women became her passion, and their tea parties were a large part of their lives. Teaching others about tea parties has become a full-time ministry for Frannie. "I'm supposed to help people get back into this thing that we're all very special. I have never met a person yet that is not special in some way, shape, or form. Nobody is inferior," she said. A piece of Victorian philosophy that she passes along is as follows: Know your assets. That's what you enter a room with—not your debits (you're a fool if you do).

Frannie Norton

Frannie believes that when Queen Victoria died in 1901, the Victorian culture was gradually squeezed out by rougher times. She speaks of the World War II days when women joined the work force to support the war. "When a woman had to go out of her life—out of her element of beauty—and into a harsher existance, she lost the creative aspects of life. I try to tell women that they are unique individuals, and anything they do is fabulous. We women are the crème à la crème! My memories are of women. Women are the 'pretty part' of childhood. The Victorians believed God put women on earth to be caretakers of beauty."

She feels that today's cocktail party replaced the Victorian tea party. However, with stronger enforcement of drunk driving laws and alcohol's new status as a drug; she says people are searching for alternative ways to socialize and have fun. "It's really the camaraderie. It's getting together that's more important now than ever."

Frannie's job is to guide women through the planning and execution of tea parties. "The idea of giving a tea scares them, They think, like I used to think, that giving a tea is something really hard to do." She goes to the home or facility a woman or group has chosen for the tea party, finding out what the host hopes to accomplish with the party and makes suggestions for menus, arrangement of the room and service line, recommendations for table appointments, etc. She teaches the hostesses subtle history lessons about Victorian customs—about receiving lines and the Victorian love of playing dress-up. She teaches her philosophy that perfection stands in the way of a lot of things and stresses that "there are no mistakes." She reminds them that as hostesses, they **are** the party, and encourages them to be creative, adventuresome party givers. "I show them that there are no rules. It's your party. Victorians would never invite anyone to their parties that they were not comfortable with. The main thing at the party is friendship."

Wheaton, Illinois 185

Frannie assists with tea parties for churches, groups, individuals, and retail establishments in the DuPage County area of Illinois. She gives presentations each month in Geneva, Illinois, at a well-known store called the Little Traveler.

Besides being a well-known historian of Victorian teas, crafts, and customs, Frannie is also the author and self publisher of a book called *A Victorian Cup of Tea*. It includes history about the Victorian tea party, ideas for authentic theme teas, and her favorite tea recipes, and is available at stores in the DuPage county suburbs or directly from her (see Illinois Tea Room directory).

She related a story about a Christian woman who became upset at one of her book signings when she mentioned the Victorian love of tea leaf reading. She explained to the woman that Victorians were highly spiritual people. She'd found no evidence in her research that pointed to any disrespect of their faith. She said, "The Victorian hostess wanted to make sure you went away happier than when you came. They always invited people to teas that they adored. If a hostess noticed that a friend was down, she'd read the depressed friend's tea leaves. She'd take a spoon to rearrange the tea leaves to fit the problem and turn it around for a positive flow. It was to lift your spirits—to bring you joy. It was used as a tool to make a friend happy."

Frannie heartily applies what she teaches others to her own life. She invited me to her home for our meeting and proceeded to make me feel like a very special guest. Although we were having a business meeting of sorts, she had set the table with an informal afternoon tea spread. She explained that her dishes were the old American Sweetheart pattern that her mother collected as premiums from the movie theater. They were the special dishes used only at birthdays for service of her mother's homemade chocolate cake. She'd created a lovely little sign for our tea table that said:

Sunshine
Pink giggles
Smiles
Friendship

When I asked her about the sign, she answered simply, "Why that's our day!"

Frannie is very hopeful about the future of tea parties in the Midwest. She feels that we're just on the cutting edge of the "tea thing" that has captured the hearts of Americans in other regions of the country.

"It's a simple thing," she said. "And it's the simple things in life that make you happy." She seems to have grabbed onto life's brass ring. It's little wonder she signs her books and letters "Victoriously yours."

Wheaton, Illinois

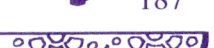

AMY'S FORGOTTEN COOKIES

2 egg whites
2/3 cup sugar
1 cup chocolate or butterscotch chips
1/2 cup chopped walnuts (optional)
pinch of salt

Beat egg whites until soft peaks form. Add sugar and salt, a tablespoon at a time, until stiff and shiny. Fold in chocolate bits and nuts. Drop by teaspoons onto ungreased cookie sheets. Place in a 350° fully preheated oven and immediately turn off heat, and forget the cookies until the next morning or at least four hours before opening the oven door. Do not for **any** reason, open the oven door before four hours are over. Makes about 48 cookies.

Frannie says, "Once you meet Amy, like the song, you are always in love with Amy. She's that kind of girl—a true Victorian lady. This recipe is very simple. It's a darling cookie. She's given the recipe away a million times." Amy and Frannie worked together at the museum.

AUNT EILEEN'S POUND CAKE

1 cup margarine
2 cups granulated sugar
4 eggs
3 cups flour
1 1/2 teaspoon baking powder
1 teaspoon lemon extract
1 cup milk
1 teaspoon mace

Cream shortening; and add sugar a little at a time, creaming again. Add one egg at a time, beating well after each addition. Sift flour, mace, baking powder, together. Add lemon extract to the milk. Add alternately the flour mixture, then the milk mixture to the shortening mixture ending with the flour as the last addition. Pour into a greased and floured 10-inch tube pan. Bake 90 minutes in a 325° preheated oven.

This is the recipe that Frannie's husband, Johnny, votes is her very best. He recommended that she donate it to share with you readers.

VERN DU PLAIN, TEA LECTURER
CRYSTAL LAKE, ILLINOIS

Afternoon tea commenced in the backyard of a friend's house leaving a six year old Chicago girl with an impression to last a lifetime. Vern Du Plain can remember that playtime was put on hold when her friend's mother carried a tray outside laden with saltine crackers spread with strawberry jam and a pot of lukewarm tea. "I thought-Wow!" laughed Vern. She often sprinkles her subject with personal antecdotes when she speaks to groups about the romance of tea.

She can't remember that her family partook in afternoon tea, but her mother often required Vern's company at "ladies' luncheons" hosted by her friends. The memorable feature of those events was the array of pound cakes that were served for dessert before the children guests were dismissed for play. "There was a lot of one-upsmanship going on in those days," she recalled. The ladies' luncheons were a time when the hostess used her best table appointments and culinary skills.

A former counselor specializing in relationship and career stress, Vern had always been interested in antiques and Victorianna. *Victorian* magazine was a big influence on her choice to make a career change. She loved to lose herself between the pages that portrayed a gentle lifestyle frosted with romance and beauty. "You can not let go of stress easily," she said. "Stress does not leave at 5:00 p.m. People need to slow down. They're dying of stress. We were put here to enjoy. Gestalt therapy says 'let the child come up and play.' When do children play a lot? At tea parties! It lets the child come out." After years in a career of traveling to teach seminars, etc., Vern was ready to go out and play.

She and I agree strongly about the misconceptions people have of tea being a very stuffy thing. "They think tea is something only the Queen could pull off. Tea parties are for communication. You can serve tea in a cracked cup, and it will still be very enjoyable," she said. "Women have a special relationship with each other that needs to be shared. If you put everything on a pretty little plate or napkin and serve it with some graciousness—it's tea."

Vern says the ingredients for a successful tea party are hospitality and conversation. "The more I see of tea, the more convinced I am that you can't go wrong. You can take cookies out of a package and put them on a plate with a doily and then hide the package." Food quality is important, but there is no need for it to be homemade or fussy. "I could go into anyone's refrigerator and pull out something to serve at tea," she said. (Now, there I might be doubtful. When I was single, I only went to the store when I was out of laundry detergent or cat food. I'm certain there are a few readers who could share even more pathetic stories.)

A gifted speaker, Vern can present a program that lasts 15 minutes or two hours. She shares her thoughts, experiences, and tips about serving tea to a wide variety of civic groups and audiences in retail tea establishments. The audience always seems to be mesmerized by her simple message of "hospitali-tea." She relates stories about her tea experiences in Great Britain and the Orient. She provides listeners with practical ways to add instant cachet to tea time and to make being a tea hostess an enjoyable, non-stressful affair. Her tips for garnishing, sandwich making, and baking "the world's best scones" are devoured by all. There are usually plenty of questions, and guests get a chance to share some of their tea experiences.

Vern is apparently listening to herself when she speaks. She has three daughters living nearby. They have tea together often in plumply padded, wicker chairs in her sunroom that is decorated in an ivy motif. "My four year old granddaughter loves tea parties. It must be in the genes. And don't sell little boys short. They love to have tea, but they all want to pour." A tea table is set and ready for service at all times in her family room—she just adds hot water and scones. Even her laundry room has a tea theme with a perky collection of tea pots she's collected over the years.

Crystal Lake, Illinois

"The tea spirit is the essence of life," she maintains. "Tea is not everyone's thing, but everyone should experience it just once. And they might get hooked!" After all, as she puts it, "Tea is a love affair with beautiful things and pleasantries from end to end. It's a romantic ceremony." Who could resist the restorative value of a nice "cuppa" tea?

ENGLISH FRUIT

Place in a large baking dish:
1-16 ounce can apricot halves, drained
1-16 ounce can Elberta peach halves, drained
1-16 ounce can Bartlett pear halves, drained
1-16 ounce can pineapple chunks, drained

Sprinkle the fruit with:
1/2 cup brown sugar
2-3 tablespoons butter (cut in small pieces)
nutmeg
cinnamon

Bake 1 hour at 350° uncovered, and serve hot.

Doesn't this dish sound like it would make wonderful breakfast tea fare? It would be a good side dish for a tea luncheon too.

For a plate or tea tray garnish, Vern suggests thinning a bit of marshmallow creme with water. Brush with a pastry brush on a small clump of grapes. Sprinkle with sugar and refrigerate.

THE WALNUT STREET TEA COMPANY
CHAMPAIGN, ILLINOIS

Although I was under the impression that the revival of tea drinking is a rather recent phenomena, Betty Elliot of the Walnut Street Tea Company, knows much better—she has all the facts. It was over twelve years ago that she (seeking a career change) and two former partners opened the quaint little tea shop at a busy intersection in downtown Champaign.

I was first attracted to this tea store (**it's not a tea room**) before my burgeoning career as a tea room author launched itself. I was drawn to it because its tiled exterior conjures up images of how I thought a tea shop should look—much like a little English proprietorship. And a beautiful display of delicate, floral, china tea cups never fails to escape my eye. It's a precious place that's run by an entrepreuner who knows her business and her customers.

Over the years, Betty has noticed trends in her tea market. "Customers are more knowledgeable now," she said. "They have tried the less expensive, poorer quality, supermarket products. They are dissatisfied and have come back to quality." A bad economy, she says, is fuel for her retail fire because she sells simple, inexpensive luxuries that people can still afford to treat themselves to. They may not be able to afford European vacations; but they can enjoy foods with European flavors such as their favorite teas, coffees, shortbreads, sweets, etc. She says she sells about equal proportions of loose teas and bag teas.

There is a very sizable foreign population in Champaign due to the influx of people to the University of Illinois. These people drink large amounts of tea, she says; and they buy loose teas by the pound (that's a **lot** of tea).

A scandalous variety of teaphernalia is amassed on the shelves of the tiny Walnut Street Tea Company. Bulk herbs, spices, and teas are available; and the popularity of flavored coffees has caused Betty to devote a goodly amount of floor space to tubs of

Champaign, Illinois

beans. You can imagine the smells that waft through the shop's air. There are gourmet items of all kinds, plenty of teatime shortbreads and crackers, a wide selection of teapots, china, and brewing apparatus. There are books, tea canisters, tins, and decorative accessories. It's one charming little place.

Betty crafts many gift baskets—especially during holiday times. Any time of the year is the right time for a customized gift basket that can be made to suit individual tastes and makes gift giving easier for the hard-to-buy-for recipient.

The personality of this tea shop owner, like many of the tea room owners in this book, is one of dedication to customer service. There are many repeat customers who have become frequent shoppers in her store. People appreciate being waited on by a person who can make recommendations, answer questions, and cares that they are there.

The excellent, visable location near downtown shops and art galleries encourages walk-by business, and the one-way street lends for easy parking access. The tea store is a hubbub of activity.

If you have reason to be in the Champaign area (located at the intersection of Interstates 57 and 74 in central Illinois), and are besotted by the tea bug; I urge you to tarry a moment at the convivial Walnut Street Tea Company.

Recipe Index

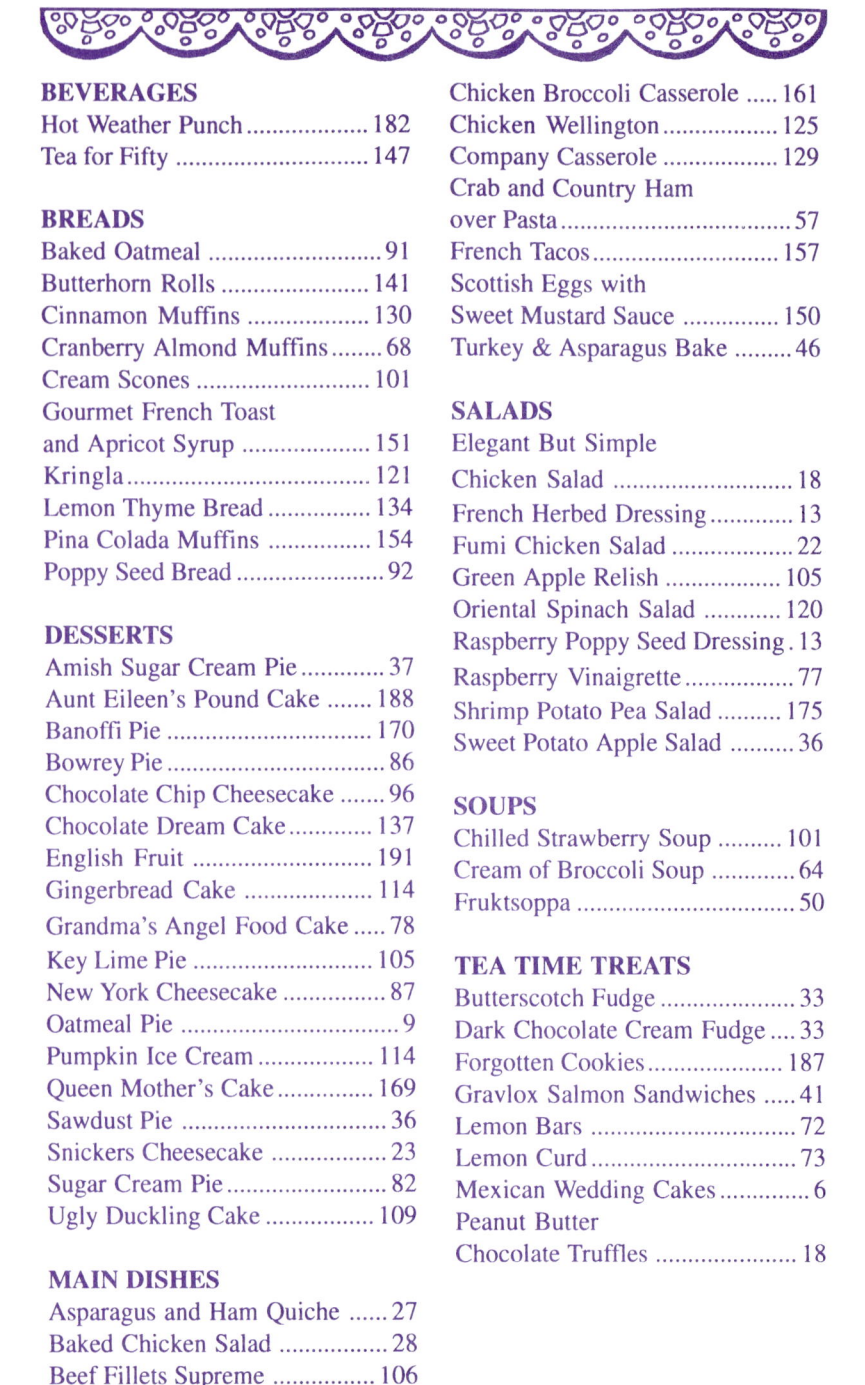

BEVERAGES
Hot Weather Punch 182
Tea for Fifty 147

BREADS
Baked Oatmeal 91
Butterhorn Rolls 141
Cinnamon Muffins 130
Cranberry Almond Muffins 68
Cream Scones 101
Gourmet French Toast
and Apricot Syrup 151
Kringla 121
Lemon Thyme Bread 134
Pina Colada Muffins 154
Poppy Seed Bread 92

DESSERTS
Amish Sugar Cream Pie 37
Aunt Eileen's Pound Cake 188
Banoffi Pie 170
Bowrey Pie 86
Chocolate Chip Cheesecake 96
Chocolate Dream Cake 137
English Fruit 191
Gingerbread Cake 114
Grandma's Angel Food Cake 78
Key Lime Pie 105
New York Cheesecake 87
Oatmeal Pie 9
Pumpkin Ice Cream 114
Queen Mother's Cake 169
Sawdust Pie 36
Snickers Cheesecake 23
Sugar Cream Pie 82
Ugly Duckling Cake 109

MAIN DISHES
Asparagus and Ham Quiche 27
Baked Chicken Salad 28
Beef Fillets Supreme 106

Chicken Broccoli Casserole 161
Chicken Wellington 125
Company Casserole 129
Crab and Country Ham
over Pasta 57
French Tacos 157
Scottish Eggs with
Sweet Mustard Sauce 150
Turkey & Asparagus Bake 46

SALADS
Elegant But Simple
Chicken Salad 18
French Herbed Dressing 13
Fumi Chicken Salad 22
Green Apple Relish 105
Oriental Spinach Salad 120
Raspberry Poppy Seed Dressing . 13
Raspberry Vinaigrette 77
Shrimp Potato Pea Salad 175
Sweet Potato Apple Salad 36

SOUPS
Chilled Strawberry Soup 101
Cream of Broccoli Soup 64
Fruktsoppa 50

TEA TIME TREATS
Butterscotch Fudge 33
Dark Chocolate Cream Fudge 33
Forgotten Cookies 187
Gravlox Salmon Sandwiches 41
Lemon Bars 72
Lemon Curd 73
Mexican Wedding Cakes 6
Peanut Butter
Chocolate Truffles 18

Illinois Tea Room Directory

Cafe Las Bellas Artes Ltd.
112 West Park Avenue
Elmhurst, Illinois, 60126
Gloria Duarte
800-530-CAFE
708-530-7725

Cedar Pointe Tea Room
#2 Cedar Street
Pana, Illinois, 62557
Bill & Judy Clawson
Lisa Goatley, Tea Room Mgr.
217-562-4554

Country Thyme Tea Room
931 S. Railroad
Paxton, Illinois, 60957
Bonnie Kaeb
217-379-4748

**The Dicus House
Bed & Breakfast**
609 E. Broadway St.
Streator, Illinois, 61364
Art & Felicia Bucholtz
815-672-6700

Frannie Norton
1012 N. Wheaton Ave.
Wheaton, Illinois, 60187
708-665-0249

The Garden Room
809 N. Main
Princeton, Illinois, 61358
Bonnie Cuffe
Darlene Johnson
815-875-1706

International Tea Source
438 Robert Parker Rd.
Long Grove, Illinois, 60047
John Mendez
708-821-7006

International Tea Source
3324 North Halsted
Chicago, Illinois, 60657
Barbara Mendez
312-665-4393

Jefferson Hill Tea Room
43 E. Jefferson Ave.
Naperville, Illinois, 60540
Kris Guill
708-420-8521

Pinehill Bed & Breakfast
400 Mix Street
Oregon, Illinois 61061
Sharon Burdick
815-732-2061

Illinois Tea Room Directory

Raspberry Tea Room
Rt. 51
Elwin, Illinois, 62532
Jeanette Ball
Virginia Bilyeu
217-865-2916

Seasons of Long Grove
314 Old McHenry Road
Long Grove, Illinois, 60047
John Wise
708-634-9150

The Spicery Tea Room
Main & Scott St.
Tuscola, Illinois, 61953
Donna Kidwell
217-253-5091

The Tea Party Cafe
113 E. State Street
Geneva, Illinois, 60134
Lucinda Williams
708-208-6844

Tiara Manor Tea Room
403 West Court Street
Paris, Illinois, 61944
Jo Marie Nowarita
1-800-531-1865
217-465-1865]

Vern Du Plain
6610 Deerwood Dr.
Crystal Lake, Illinois, 60012
815-459-8628

Walnut Street Tea Co.
115 S. Walnut
Champaign, Illinois, 61820
Betty Elliot
217-351-6975

Windowpanes Tea Room
Inn on the Square
Oakland, Illinois, 61943
Gary & Linda Miller
217-346-2289

Indiana Tea Room Directory

Almost Home Inc.
17 West Franklin St.
Greencastle, Indiana, 46135
Gail Carrington
Sara Malayer
317-653-5788

The Good Stuff
219 E. Center
Warsaw, Indiana, 46580
Mallory Miniear
219-269-6500

The Queen Anne Inn
420 West Washington St.
South Bend, Indiana, 46601
Bob & Pauline Medhurst
800-582-2379
219-234-5959

Rose Arbor Tea Room
110 Lincolnway East
Mishawaka, Indiana, 46544
Lynett Heritz
219-254-0121

Story Inn
6404 South SR 135
Nashville, Indiana, 47448
Bob & Gretchen Haddix
812-988-2273

The Tea Room
500 S. Main
Elkhart, Indiana, 46515
Jan Myers
Cindy Donnellson
219-522-9496

Trolley Cafe
The Old Bag Factory
1100 Chicago Ave.
Goshen, Indiana, 46526
Aaron Hoober
219-534-3881

The Victorian Guest House
302 East Market Street
Nappanee, Indiana, 46550
Bruce & Vickie Hunsberger
219-773-4383

Iowa Tea Room Directory

Barkley House
Bed & Breakfast
326 Boone Street
Boone, Iowa, 50036
David & Rosella Hanson
800-753-8586
515-432-7885

Bette Dryer's
Tea Room & Catering
107 East Salem
Indianola, Iowa, 50125
Bette Dryer
515-961-7116

The Blue Onion Tea Room
210 N. Main
Roland, Iowa, 50236
Mary Ann Anderson
515-388-4858

Blue Willow Tea Room
Highway 169 East
Harcourt, Iowa, 50544
Connie Gustafson
515-354-5295

The Brandenburg
215 East Bremer Avenue
Waverly, Iowa, 50677
Cynthia L. Shipman
319-352-5066

The Carousel
Tea Room & Bakery
619 Elm
Story City, Iowa, 50248
Candice L. Anderson
800-765-4280
515-733-2388

Cottage Sampler
Tea Room
324 W. 4th St.
St. Ansgar, Iowa, 50472
Judy Goplerud
515-736-4484

The Country Porch
Box 78
127 E. Main
Hawkeye, Iowa, 52147
Marilyn Niewoehner
Ruthie Smith
319-427-3377

Diekman Mercantile
107 S. State
Denver, Iowa, 50622
Steve & Marie Nowak
319-984-6258

The Douglass House
721 Carrol Street
Boone, Iowa, 50036
Joleen Muench
515-432-4078

Iowa Tea Room Directory

Emma's Tea Room
519 Court St.
Williamsburg, Iowa, 52361
Joan Heitman
Elaine Wardenburg
319-668-1849

Just A Bite Tea House
5282 Apricot Lane, Box 32
Emmons, Minnesota, 56029
Becky Aalgaard
Bobbie Coulter
Donna Hall
515-293-JAVA

Martha's Coffee Station
119 South 4th Street
Cherokee, Iowa, 51012
Margaret Woltman
Becky Patterson
712-225-4664

One of a Kind Tea Room
314 West State
Centerville, Iowa, 52544
Jack & Joyce Stufflebeem
515-437-4540

Tea Thyme at Sadie's
2021 6th Ave. South
Fort Dodge, Iowa, 50501
Debra Lacina
515-576-2202

The Owl House
410 Antique City Drive
Walnut, Iowa, 51577
Carol Rosenbaum
712-784-2229

Thymes Remembered Tea Room
1 St and Otley
Perry, Iowa, 50220
Ramona Birdsell
515-465-2631

Wisconsin Tea Room Directory

Bits of Britain
1201 E. Russell St.
Milwaukee, Wisconsin, 53207
June Gray &
Diane Edwardsen
414-744-3989

**Bits of Britain &
A Wee Bit More**
294 W. Main St.
Waukesha, Wisconsin, 53186
June Gray &
Diane Edwardsen
414-896-7772

**New Glarus Bakery &
Tea Room**
534 First Street
New Glarus, Wisconsin, 53574
Howard & Nancy Weber
608-527-2916

**The Victorian Belle
Boutique & Tea Room**
Old Theater Mall
169 East Wisconsin Ave.
Oconomowoc, Wisconsin,
53006
Barb Jaeger
414-567-3990

Tea Stuff

Tea people need to find their "tea stuff." The following is a list of some tea rooms, luncheon rooms, tea shops and gift shops that appear to be of interest to tea lovers. Some have been recommended by others; some I have found through research. I've even visited a few of them. I certainly wish I had time & space to let you know more about each one.

Remember-Always call ahead to verify hours of operation. Almost all of these places are managed by entrepreneurs who have the right to change their agendas at any time. Happy tea trails!

The Pleasure's Been Mine,
Joyce Decherd

Illinois

Anna Lee's Tea Room
223 E. Livingston
Monticello
217-762-5456

Aunt Mandy's Tea Room
West side of Public Square
Petersburg
217-632-2643

The Back Porch Tea Room
108 N. Main
Washington
309-444-8379

The Black Dog Café
105 N. Franklin
Polo, IL. 61064
815-946-3591

The Blue Parrot
Riverside
708-447-2233

The Buttery
Wilmette

Carroll place
110 W. Market St.
Mt. Carroll
815-244-2166

Clover Patch Cafe
406 S. Schuyler St.
Lena
815-369-5174

Country Dumpling Tea Room
1295 Peoria St.
Washington

Country Pantry Tea Room
132 McKinley
East Peoria
309-694-1972

The Country Touch & Tea Room
105 N. Main St.
Atwood
217-578-3214

Court Street Tea Room
500 South Court St.
Marion
618-997-4883

Elsah's Landing Bakery & Tea Room
18-20 LaSalle St.
The Elsah Landing, IL
618-374-1607

The Front Street Gourmet

Tea Stuff

11 W. Front
El Paso
309-527-3215

Garden Terrace Tea Room
Forrest
815-657-7070

Gourmet Junction
505 W. Lockport St.
Plainfield
815-439-3933

Gramma's House
311 N. Aldrich
Geneseo
309--944-2623

The Heart of Christmas
Write 480 Richmond Lane
Crystal Lake, IL 60014
815-459-3243
November teas at Christmas event

Heartland Square Mini Mall & Tea Room
1215 S. Edwardsville St.
Staunton
618-635-2772

Heartland Tea Room
Rt 29
Chillicothe
309-274-2283
in Heartland Craft Mall

Heavenly Treasures
Locust & 8th
Delavan
309-244-8292

The Herrington Inn
15 South River Lane
Geneva
800-216-2466, 708-208-8920

Hickory Stick Gift Shops & Tea Room
419 Beech St.
Chillicothe
309-274-6078

Isch's Tea Room & Coffee House
109 W. Partridge
Metamora, Illinois
309-367-2700

Jacqueline's
27 Main
Oswego
708-554-3265

The Little Traveler
404 S. 3rd St.
Geneva
708-232-4200

Lutz Continental Cafe & Pastry Shop
2458 West Montrose
Chicago
312-478-7785
Viennese Coffee & Pastries

Maison Gourmet
907 Burlington
Western Springs
708-246-0002

Main Street Cafe & Tea Room
1414 Broadway
Mattoon
217-235-4733

Margarita Inn
1566 Oak Ave.
Evanston
708-869-2273

Mari-Mann's Herb Co. Inc.
Decatur
217-429-1404
Lunches (Thursdays) and
Teas for groups by reservation

The Mustard Seed
208 N. Main
Morton
309-263-1046

Tea Stuff

My Flower Garden Bakery & Tea Room
2670 W. Jefferson
Springfield
217-546-6373

Oak Brook Hills Resort
3500 Midwest Rd.
Westmont
708-850-5555
Afternoon Teas

Old Oak Creek Tea Room
Rt. 34 & 71
Oswego
708-554-3218

The Picket Fence Tea Room
22 E. Elm
Canton
309-647-7437

Pleasant Hill Antique Mall & Tea Room
315 S. Pleasant Hill Rd.
East Peoria
309-694-4040
In an antique mall

Punky's Palace Tea Room
155 Frontage Rd.
North of Farmersville
Antique Mall & Mansion

Raspberry Tea Room
1661 North Main St.
Princeton
815-872-2580
Sherwood Antique Mall

Russian Tea Time
63 East Adams St.
Chicago
312-360-0000
Former Soviet Republics Cuisine,
Russian Tea from the Samovar

Susan's Tea Room
North Side of Square
309-444-8999
Washington

Sweet Annie's Courtyard
(On the Square)
Shelbyville

Sweet Buns
Main & 3rd
Vermont
309-784-2510

Tea for Two
112 S. Main
Eureka
309-467-2555

The Tearose Tea Room
403 N. Western Ave.
Peoria
309-676-7460

The Terrace Tea Room & Bakery
611 E. State
Jacksonville
217-243-1319

Todd & Holland Tea Merchants
417 Lathrop Ave.
River Forrest
708-488-1136
Fine Estate Teas-Mail Order only

Toni Marie's
51 S. Washington
Hinsdale
708-789-2020

The Village Tea Room
110 S. Main
Washington
309-444-7084
Behind Tea Time & Treasures

The Walnut Tree House Tea Room
112 West Main St.
Knoxville
309-289-6933
(also a B&B)

Wheaton History Center
606 North Main St.
Wheaton
708-682-9472
Annual January Theme Tea

Indiana

Clarinda's Cottage
Tearoom and Gift Shop
Number 3 Market St.
Newburgh

The Columbus Inn
445 5th St.
Columbus
Afternoon Teas

Gramma and Grampa's
Fremont
219-495-1751

The Greenfield Herb Garden
Depot and Harrison
Shipshewana
Seasonal Theme Teas

The Herb Garden
Unique Restaurant
West Side of the Square
Rockville
317-569-6055

The Jenny Wren
Mooresville
Seasonal Afternoon Teas

The Looking Glass Tea Room in Reflections Gift Shop
330 East Main St.
Plainfield
317-839-0899
Lunches and Afternoon Teas

Me and Ewe
522 E. National Ave.
Brazil
812-448-1600

Patti's Place
103 1/2 West Joliet St.
Crown Point
219-663-6344

Somewhere in Thyme
4201 S. 7th
Terea Haute
812-235-0883
Lunch by reservation

Silver Spoon Tea Room
211 S. Main
Zionsville
317-873-0911
English Luncheons & Afternoon Teas
In the Butlers Pantry

Victorianna's
211 Van Buren St.
812-988-1128
Nashville
Monthly afternoon teas

Wisconsin

American Club
Kohler
800-344-2838
Holiday Afternoon Teas
Call for other times

The Inn at Cedar Crossing
Sturgeon Bay
414-743-4200
Tea Time on special occasions

George Watts and Son, Inc.
761 N. Jefferson St.
Milwaukee
414-291-5120 or 800-747-9288
Lunches and Afternoon Tea

Pilgrim Square Tea Room
2300 Pilgrim Road
Near Milwaukee
414-784-4556
Lunches

Primrose Tea Room
N88W16733 Appleton Ave.
Menomonee Falls

Tea Stuff

Iowa

Apple Alley Tea Room
421 Main
Bedford
712-523-2073
Antique Mall & Spec. Shops

Aunt Beas's Tea & Gifts
607 College St.
Marble Rock
515-397-2244

Cappuccino's Gourmet
Cafe and Sweet Shop
1620 W. First St.
Ankeny
515-965-8894

Chestnut Tree
222 Chestnut
Atlantic
712-243-3902

The Country Inn & Briar Patch
109 W. Center
Conrad
515-366-2226

Daisy's Tea Room
726 N. Main @ Minchen House
Carroll
712-792-3849

de Snoepwinkel
605 Franklin
Pella
515-628-1222

Fernhill
Hwy 6 and 220
South Amana
319-622-3627
Beverages and Desserts

The Gift Box Front Porch Cafe
1010 Main
Manson
712-469-3874

The Hampton House of Special "Teas"
115 1st NW
Hampton
515-456-4842

Heirloom Treasures & Tea Room
411 Bluff St.
Dubuque
319-557-8072

In Good Company
825 Shakespeare
Stratford
515-838-2750

Ivy's Shoppes on Grand
6th and Grand
Ames
515-232-0275

Lake Coffee House and Cottage Treasures
412 North Shore Drive
Clear Lake
515-357-5700

Little Meeting House
107 Cerro Gordo St.
Rock Falls
Lunches by Reservation
515-696-5669

Memory Lane Treasures Teahouse
Wright Bros. Rd.
Cedar Rapids
319-848-7275
Lunches by Reservation

Mansion Antiques Tea Room and Gift Shop
307 4th St.
Malcom
515-528-5300
Lunches by Reservation

Olde Town Antiques & Tea Room
121 S.E. 2nd St.
Altoona
515-967-7770

Tea Stuff

"Pastimes" in the Heiman House
518 N. Main
Buffalo Center
515-562-2513
Lunch by Reservation, Tea Time

The Peppercorn Pantry
911 Parrot
Aplington
319-347-2797

Rachel's Tea Room
408 Elm St.
Eldon
515-652-3338

Remember When
225 N. Aker
Latimer
515-579-6208

Scandia Imports & Tearoom
506 Kellogg
Ames
515-232-0548

Shar B's
1420 Market St.
Burlington
319-754-6159
Lunches & teas by reservation

Special Thymes
204 Antique City Dr.
Walnut
712-784-3050

Sugar Tree
312 Main
Ames
515-232-3442

The Tea Garden
100 E. State
Jefferson
515-386-3888

Victorian Garden Tea Room
116 W. Main St.
Marshalltown
515-753-4963

Victoria's By the Park
323 West 2nd St.
Cedar Falls

Village Tea Room & Treasures
706 N. Barnes St.
What Cheer
515-634-2115

Vivian's Tea Room
121 High Ave East
Oskaloosa

Woodbine Tea Room
418 Walker St.
Woodbine
800-297-1208 or 647-2803

Wood 'n What Not Tea Room
1043 Sunset Dr.
Norwalk
515-981-5065

Younker's Tea Room
Seventh & Walnut
Des Moines
515-247-7161

My Tea Friends & Me

MY TEA FRIENDS AND ME

The great "sisterhood of tea" never ceases to amaze me. We understand what tea is about. More than anything else, it's a sharing of the spirit of hospitali-tea that invades other areas of our lives.

The main characteristic we have in common is that we love to share all we know about tea and tea rooms. A good example of this is my relationship with Judy Harris, the designer of this book. Judy and I collect piles of designated "tea stuff" in our houses to show each other. When the stacks become unbearably deep, we arrange a show and tell session. We share tea catalogs, books, recipes, newspaper clippings, tea room sightings, tea greeting cards we have found, etc., etc.—all over a cup of tea of course! Because these sessions can be rather lengthy, we usually have tea treats designed to keep up our strength.

Letter and note writing seems to go along with the tea affliction. It's another thing of the past that we are reluctant to release. Few things in this world can compare to opening the mailbox and finding a letter. The only other experience I can compare it to is when I have a roll of film processed and I'm holding the unopened envelope of photographs in my hand. It's a tingling sensation that resurrects the feeling of excitement I felt about so many things as a child but seem to have lost over the years. Thank goodness other tea sisters understand about letters! I am so greatful for the letters I receive from readers who write and share about their favorite tea rooms.

Here, I feature recipes from some of the friends that I have met through tea, some from relatives, and a few of my own favorites. In reality, I believe that the food at tea time or luncheon is secondary. Atmosphere is important, but not critical. What really counts is service of ample portions of hospitali-tea! And each of these ladies, in her own way, does that with ease.

PAM BAYER

I met Pam when we were seated at the tea table at Victorian Special Teas in Lynnwood, Illinois. I'd be afraid to lose touch with Pam. She is such a valuable source of information and has a little different perspective on tea because of her Indiana connections. Pam is a crazy woman for tea. She currently lives in Hammond, Indiana, and dreams of opening or managing a tea room one day soon. I can't wait to be a customer!

MOSAIC SANDWICHES

4 tablespoons softened butter
4 tablespoons softened cream cheese or Neufchatel
1/2 cup grated cheddar or Monterey cheese
1 cup hard salami cut in 1/2" cubes
1 cup (3/4 pound) cubed ham or turkey
3 tablespoons pickle relish
fresh chives (to taste)
4-5 bread sticks (Cut off both ends and hollow out with handle of a wooden spoon.)

Mix butter, cream cheese, and grated cheese until smooth. Stir in the relish and chives. Add meat cubes and stir. Fill breadsticks with the meat mixture using a cookie press or a pastry bag with a large tip. Wrap in plastic wrap and refrigerate. When you are ready to serve, cut with a serrated knife into thin slices. Place on a tray, and refrigerate until serving time. (May be made the day before. Don't slice until serving day.)

Pam garnered this recipe in an English tea class taught by Hungarian-born chef, Judith Nagy Goldinger, of Crown Point, Indiana.

VERA BEGGS

Meeting Vera Beggs over the tea table at one of Frannie Norton's teas (see page 183) was one of the highlights of my tea career. I have always been one who enjoys going to restaurants, events, and shopping alone. It allows me to concentrate on the experience without distractions, and I tend to meet some of the most interesting people at those times. Although tea time is supposed to be "time-out" to spend with friends, it is also the perfect situation to make new aquaintances.

Vera, the good tea lady she is, had brought a friend from work to introduce her to the concept of a Victorian afternoon tea. My seating assignment was at their table, and it took about two minutes to figure out that Vera was as fanatical about tea as me. I think her friend was a bit mystified at this inside glimpse of "the world of tea," but she was a great sport and didn't even hint that we might be a bit wacko.

Our next tea caper was instigated when Vera called to invite me to run over to Shipshewana the next day to enjoy a "fairy tea" at the Greenfield Herb Garden........It was only three hours away—not far at all for an afternoon of tea. And we've been tea-ing together ever since.

Unlike many lovers of tea (who sip through the first courses as they try to appear nonchalant about the forthcoming dessert tray), Vera and I focus in on the first course of tea—the savories (that's sandwiches to those of you who are still trying to figure about what I'm talking about). The English spelling is savouries. I can't speak for Vera, but I can say it would be hard to overdose on tea sandwiches.

It is only fitting that I record some of Vera's favorite sandwich fillings in *Midwestern Tea Room Pleasures.*

She writes, "Among all the types of sandwiches I have tried for English tea, the following have been most successful. (There is even an egg-based choice for vegetarians.) For dessert I usually serve fresh fruits (strawberries), scones, lemon bars, lemon or banana tea bread, mini-brownies, and a fancy cake or cheesecake."

CHICKEN TARRAGON

Mix the following: cut up cooked chicken (3 cups or more), fresh or dried tarragon to taste, salt, and pepper. Use mayonnaise to bind ingredients (I use the "light" version.)

🍵 *This filling is particularly good on mini-croissants that are lined with dark, leafy greens.*

DILL & TUNA

Mix the following: 1 large can of white albacore tuna, 1 bunch green scallions (chopped), salt, and pepper. Use mayonnaise ("light or regular") to bind ingredients together.

🍵 *Try this filling on light wheat bread with the crusts removed. Top with alfalfa sprouts.*

EGG SALAD CURRY

Mix the following: 6 hard-boiled eggs (mashed), 1 bunch chopped scallions, curry powder (to taste), salt, and pepper. Use "light" or regular mayonnaise to bind.

🍵 *Mini, white rolls make a good bread for these sandwiches. I put chopped salad burnet leaves (has a cucumber taste) on top.*

SMOKED SALMON

1-4 ounce package smoked salmon
1-8 ounce package cream cheese, softened
sliced tomatoes
scallions, chopped
dill weed (fresh if possible)
salt and pepper
mini-bagels, sliced in half

Spread the cream cheese on the mini bagel halves. Add smoked salmon. Top with sliced tomatoes, chopped scallions, and fresh dill, salt, and pepper (if desired).

ANN DECHERD

One of my very best sources of recipes is my mother-in-law, Ann Decherd of Zanesville, Ohio. She has always loved to bake and entertain, but has not had much opportunity until her recent retirement from school teaching. Now she plays hostess at every opportunity. Last summer I was able to spend a week in Ohio. It appears to be a state with plenty of opportunities for tea room sleuthing.

PARTY SANDWICH LOAF

1 loaf round, unsliced bread (white, wheat or rye)

Slice the loaf horizontally into 3 or 4 slices. Make one layer of each: chicken salad, cheese salad, egg salad. (You may substitute tuna salad or ham salad.) Spread each layer with a salad mixture and restack to form the shape of the loaf.
Soften 8 ounces of cream cheese (the amount depends on the size of your loaf), and stir in milk to make a spreadable "frosting."

You may tint the cream cheese mixture with food coloring. Frost the loaf. Slice into wedges for service.

You can imagine that this loaf would like nice on a tea buffet table garnished in many ways. I could see a pink or yellow loaf decorated with violets! Imagine the possibilities...

JOYCE DECHERD

In general, I'm a cook that likes to experiment at every chance. For some reason, that doesn't seem to be the case when I prepare tea for friends. I prefer to fix my favorite standards and concentrate on the presentation and garnishing. That way I don't have any concerns about the food and get to enjoy the more satisfying segments of afternoon tea. I especially love to serve tea on china and serving pieces that I don't use for everyday purposes. Many are of antique or collectible vintage that I have picked up for a few dollars on my travels because they looked "fun." I always make certain I invite an interesting selection of guests who I know will enjoy each other's company.

DILL SPREAD

1 cup mayonnaise
1 cup sour cream
2 1/4 teaspoons dried dill weed
2 1/4 teaspoons parsley flakes
2 1/4 teaspoons finely diced fresh onion
1/4 teaspoon salt
1/2 teaspoon celery salt

Mix together all ingredients until well blended. Keep refrigerated until needed.

I collected this recipe when I lived in Cedar Rapids, Iowa. I swear—Cedar Rapids must be the dill dip capital of the world! It was a standard on most deli sandwiches and many hamburgers. You could be crucified in Cedar Rapids if you served a deli buffet without dill spread. I remember when I was planning a catering event after I moved to Illinois. I asked which employee usually made the dill dip. They looked at me strangely. And I never had a customer request it. They don't seem to use it much in the Chicago area either.

Cucumber sandwiches would be excellent with dill dip. I'd recommend using thinly sliced party bread. Slice off the crusts and spread with butter (not margarine). Spread with dill dip. Peel a cucumber that has been sitting at room temperature and slice as thinly as possible. Place a slice (or arrange cucumber slice halves) on the dill dip. Top with a sprinkle of dill weed or a fresh dill.

Dill spread is also makes chicken salad special. Substitute it for plain mayonnaise. Of course, it also makes an excellent vegetable dip.

FAVORITE LETTUCE SALAD

Dressing:
1/2 cup salad oil
3/4 cup sugar
1/3 cup cider vinegar
1 teaspoon prepared mustard
1 small onion chopped finely
1 tablespoon poppy seed
dash of salt

Place all ingredients in a pint jar, and shake well. Refrigerate until use. Shake again before serving.

Pour this over your favorite lettuce or fresh spinach. The addition of cashews and Swiss cheese right before serving makes a flavor combination that's hard to beat. It's also very good with strawberry slices, shredded cheddar cheese, and sunflower seeds.

I first had this at a church potluck. Now, I keep a jar of it on hand in the refrigerator at all times. The tastes of the dressing seem to go well with many flavors. I notice guests dipping fruit, meat, bread sticks, etc. into the leftover dressing in their salad bowls to get the last drop. This is a perfect recipe to serve at a special luncheon.

IOWA CHOCOLATE CAKE

3/4 cup margarine
2 cups sugar
1 1/2 cups boiling water
2 cups flour
2 teaspoons soda

1/2 cup cocoa powder
1/2 teaspoon salt
2 eggs
1 teaspoon vanilla

Place margarine and sugar in a large mixing bowl and cover with the boiling water. In a small mixing bowl, stir the flour, soda, cocoa, and salt together. Add the dry mixture to the wet mixture, and then add the eggs and vanilla. After all the ingredients are in the bowl, beat just enough so that batter is smooth. Batter will be very thin. Pour into a greased and floured (bottom only) 9" x 13" cake pan. Bake in a preheated 350° oven for 35 to 45 minutes or done. (Edges will look like they're just ready to pull away from the pan. Be careful not to overbake. A dry chocolate cake is a sad thing.)

I'm not much of a frosting maker. I never use a recipe and just go by taste. I'd guess that I do the following: 2 cups powdered sugar, and 2 heaping tablespoons cocoa powder mixed together. Add 2 tablespoons softened margarine or butter. Add boiling water by the tablespoon until you get the desired consistency. Stir in a teaspoon of vanilla. Adjust any of the ingredients according to your own taste. Spread on a cooled cake.

This family recipe has been around for years. We had plenty of chocolate cake recipes because it was our favorite, but I have abandoned all of them in favor of this one. It is so simple that I can't see why anyone would need to use a box mix—not for chocolate cake! This one stays moist for days. If you are planning an afternoon tea or tea luncheon, it's best to plan recipes like this that you can prepare ahead of time that will remain very fresh.

JUDY HARRIS

Judy is the cover illustrator and designer of *Midwestern Tea Room Pleasures*. One of my greatest concerns when I was planning this book was finding an artist that could capture the essence of my idea of tea. I wanted feminine appeal but something that didn't seem "stuffy." After all, tea is a light-hearted thing. When I found Judy by a "chance" meeting at a craft show, the problem changed from finding an artist to limiting myself to one of her selections! The cover illustration came from a set of drawings that she had completed about seven years previously during a period of unemployment as therapy for her soul. None of the displayed drawings at the craft show had tea themes. In fact, her tea drawings were just filed away. Imagine my delight when a few days later she presented me with her portfolio! She'd been a tea and tea room lover for years. If you are a tea person, Judy is a great player to have on your tea-m!

AUNT MILDRED'S COOKIES
(Before Mrs. Fields Was Even a Twinkle in Her Father's Eye)

1 cup butter	1 teaspoon baking soda
1 1/2 cup brown sugar	1/2 cup walnut pieces
2 eggs	1/2 cup shredded coconut
1 teaspoon vanilla extract	1 cup rolled oats
2 cups flour	1 pound cut-up dates

(Use some to lightly coat the dates with flour.)

Cream butter, brown sugar, eggs, and vanilla. Sift flour and baking soda together in a separate bowl. Add walnuts, coconut, and rolled oats to butter mixture. Add flour mixture gradually and finally the dates. Drop from teaspoons on a cookie sheet. Bake 11 minutes in a pre-heated 375° oven or until slightly brown. Let cool 5 minutes before removing from the cookie sheet. Makes about 6 dozen.

Tea Friends

MARJORIE PATTON

Marjorie is my mother and a lady who detests tea. She lives in Sumner, Iowa, in a quiet, country home. When she was a child, she was quite sickly and was dosed regularly with cod liver oil and tea. (She has often told the story that her parents thought she was too frail to walk with the rest of the children to the country school they attended. Grandpa often put her in a gunny sack and carried her several miles to and from school.)

I grew up with the notion that tea was a very distasteful thing. I can not remember tasting tea until I was about 35 years old. There were some Earl Grey tea bags in our employee break room, and I decided to try it because I did not care for the brand of coffee we were using (vaguely reminiscent of a sweat sock as I remember). I think I severely over-brewed my tea due to lack of knowledge. It was bitter, but it was better than the coffee; and I enjoyed the process of brewing myself a special cup.

About a year ago, I was in a tea room with my mother. I asked her how long it had been since she had tasted tea. She thought it had been at least 50 years or so. After a lot of fancy talking, I persuaded her to try a sip of mine. Reluctantly, she took a sip and shuddered. I tried...

GINGERSNAP COOKIES

1 1/2 cups solid shortening or margarine
2 cups brown sugar
1/2 cup molasses
2 eggs
4 1/2 cups flour
2 teaspoons powdered ginger
2 teaspoons cinnamon
1 teaspoon cloves
4 teaspoons baking soda
1/2 teaspoon salt

Cream shortening and sugar until sugar crystals are dissolved with an electric mixer. Beat in molasses and eggs. Sift the dry ingredients into a medium bowl, and add to the wet mixture. Stir until all ingredients are mixed.

Roll into small balls—approximately walnut sized. Roll in granulated sugar, and place on a greased cookie sheet. Bake in a preheated 375° oven for approximately 12 minutes or until done.

I almost always serve these cookies for afternoon tea. I skimp on the sugar a bit so that the cookies are not very sweet (another of my mother's habits). They really complement a cup of tea. I imagine it was from Grandma's file. There is rivalry in our family over this recipe. Mother's gingersnaps always bake up thin and crispy. I use the same recipe, but mine always turn out puffy and soft. She likes mine better. It must be the mixing method, because I have made them in at least 10 ovens with the same results. Someday, we'll have to have a bake-off to solve the mystery of the gingersnaps.

JACKIE PETCHENIK

Although Jackie Petchenik is a Chicago native, she currently lives away from the "Tundra" (as she calls it) and resides in Santa Rosa, California. She had heard about *Midwestern Tea Room Pleasures* and called me before her Mother's Day trip back home and said something like "Hey! I'm a tea lady too! Let's get together." Doug & I need no urging when it comes to meeting tea people. We keep in touch phone, FAX, and letters.

Jackie is currently a graphic designer, desktop publisher and calligrapher. She is also the senior editor of a neat tea magazine published by Pearl Dexter called *Tea A Magazine* and loves to write about tea. She has her own special tea blend. More information about it can be found at the end of this article.

JACKIE'S TEA BREAD

3 eggs
1 cup oil
1 1/4 cups white sugar
3/4 cup brown sugar
1 teaspoon vanilla extract
2 cups ripe bananas, mashed*
3 cups all purpose flour
1 teaspoon baking powder
2 teaspoons cinnamon
1 teaspoon baking soda
1/2 cup walnuts**

Cream the first 6 ingredients, and sift all the dry ingredients except for the nuts. Stir the dry ingredients into the creamed mixture until all dry ingredients are wet. Do not overmix. Stir in the nuts.

Divide the batter into 2 well-greased loaf pans or 4 small loaf pans (my preference). Foil pans work well.

Bake in a preheated 350° oven for 45 minutes to 1 hour (depending on the size of your loaves and your oven) or until a toothpick test in the center of the loaf comes out clean. Be careful not to burn the breads.

Remove from heat, and cool in the pans. When cool, take a knife or spatula to release the edges and take out of the pans. Wrap in plastic wrap or foil to keep fresh. Then place in a zipper locked bag in the freezer.

* The bananas may be substituted with any mixture of fruits or vegetables such as cranberries, zucchini, carrots, mango, prunes, or berries of any kind. Experiment to be wonderfully surprised. You may want to mix 1 cup of banana and 1 cup of something else.

** The walnuts may be exchanged for your favorite nut, chocolate chips, raisins, currants or something else of your choosing. You may use up to 1 cup of this ingredient.

Note from Jackie: I am not a baker, really, but rather an excellent cook. I believe when you bake, you need to be pretty exact with the portions of ingredients. I am more creative which is easier to do in cooking and like to use a pinch of this and a pinch of that. With this recipe, I can get creative. This was originally a recipe from a friend's grandmother for zucchini bread which I have adapted as a tea bread. I have always loved banana bread or similar cake bread loaves. It is dangerous for me to make them because I can eat the whole thing at one sitting (ugh)! When I am ambitious, I bake a few recipes at a time and freeze them to keep at the ready for last minute gifts when invited out to dinner, for holiday gifts, for inclusion in gift baskets or just to have ready to imbibe when friends drop in for tea. (Just pop in the microwave for a few seconds until warm or let it defrost if you have enough time.) The bread is a pleasant change from scones or muffins to serve with tea.

I am a tea lady, you see, with my own blend of tea: Special Passion Blend. You can purchase my blend and other tea items by mail order. For more information, write to JP's, 589 Mission Blvd., Santa Rosa, CA 95409. Phone: 707.537.0300. FAX 707.537.0377.

Tea Friends

SUE ROUTLIFFE

Sue is a long-time friend of Judy Harris's and also a long-time lover of tea. She and Judy have entertained friends with some elaborate afternoon tea parties over the years. Sue has been able to show me the pictures of their tea tables and the scrumptious sounding menus. I've mentioned that tea sisters like to share. I'm grateful that Judy has shared Sue with me! They both grew up in the Chicago area. I love hearing their stories about their memories of the ladies' luncheons their mothers used to serve in the June Cleaver days. Back then, women sometimes prepared for several days to ready their homes and luncheon or tea tables for guests.

DANISH OATMEAL COOKIES

1/4 pound margarine
1/4 pound butter
1 cup powdered sugar
2 teaspoons vanilla
1 cup flour
1/2 teaspoon salt
1 cup quick oats
1 cup chopped nuts (walnuts or pecans)

Cream the margarine, butter, and powdered sugar. Add vanilla. Sift together the flour and salt, and stir into creamed mixture. Add the oats and nuts. Drop by teaspoon on ungreased cookie sheet. Bake in a 325° preheated oven for 20 minutes or until lightly browned. Using a sifter, sprinkle with additional powdered sugar when partly cooled. Makes 6 dozen.

🍵 *This recipe was given to Sue's mother by a dear bridge friend. Sue says it always receives compliments. (It did from me!)*

CAROL SALDEEN

Carol Saldeen of Champaign, Illinois, is a lover of Great Britain, tea time, gardens and gardening, and Beatrix Potter. I guess all five things are closely related, aren't they? I met Carol through the pages of *Mary Mac's TeaTimes* magazine. I noticed her name as a contributor of information in several articles. The thing that especially intrigued me was her Champaign address. I'd just moved from there and had only lived a few blocks away. I thought it was ironic that I finally had found a person from there with similar interests after I'd left the area. Now, Carol is one of my central Illinois tea connections. She is so thoughtful to send any clippings, etc. that she thinks I may have interest in. Her letters make mail time feel like Christmas.

In 1993, Carol had a tea in remembrance of Beatrix Potter's Peter Rabbit's 100th birthday (She is a member of the Beatrix Potter Society, an English organization.) Peter was born when Beatrix wrote a letter about him to a sick child. She later retrieved the letter and published it in 1902. Since that time, the *Tale of Peter Rabbit* has never been out of print and is known to children around the world.

At Carol's tea, the guests assembled in the garden, and the letter was read in honor of Beatrix Potter. The entrance to Carol's house was decorated with a large, floral arrangement in a watering can base with a Peter Rabbit garden ornament nearby. On the door was a fresh bunch of carrots with their green tops tied with a raffia bow. The tea table's centerpiece consisted of a green watering can just like the one in the *Tale of Peter Rabbit* with Peter peering over the top. Ceramic figurines of various Beatrix Potter characters were scattered about the table. Beatrix Potter's delicate illustrations graced the tea set. The napkins were hand-stitched with a Peter Rabbit and tucked into very small terra cotta pots. (The napkins were favors for the guests to use again as bread basket liners.)

The Peter Rabbit Tea Menu:
Mrs. Rabbit's Currant Scones
Strawberry Jam and Clotted Cream
The Flopsy Bunny's Fresh Blackberry Cobbler
Peter Rabbit's Cotton-tail Cookies
Chamomile, Blackberry, and English Afternoon Blend Tea

Carol's Peter Rabbit Tea sounds lovely. She included the basic parts of a proper afternoon tea: theme decorations, a short program, decorations to carry out the theme, guest souvenirs, and a menu representative of her topic. (This kind of tea is known as a cream tea which is served in many areas in England. It generally consists of scones with jam, clotted cream, sweets, and plenty of tea. Since access to authentic clotted cream is difficult in America, you may make your own by folding sour cream and a bit of powdered sugar into real whipped cream or use whipped topping with sour cream added.)

THE FLOPSY BUNNY'S FRESH BLACKBERRY COBBLER

3/4 cup sugar
1 tablespoon cornstarch
1 cup boiling water
3 cups fresh blackberries (Include any juice on them.)
1/2 tablespoon butter or oleo
1/2 teaspoon cinnamon

Mix together in a saucepan sugar and cornstarch. Gradually stir in boiling water. Bring to a boil, and stir while boiling for 1 minute. Add blueberries and any juice on them. Pour into a 10" x 6" x 2" baking dish. Dot with butter or oleo, and sprinkle with cinnamon. Add topping.

Topping:
1 cup flour
2 tablespoons sugar
1 1/2 teaspoons baking powder
1/4 teaspoon salt
1/4 cup butter or oleo
1 slightly beaten egg
1/4 cup milk

Mix flour, sugar, baking powder, and salt. Cut in the butter or oleo. In a separate bowl, slightly beat the egg, and add 1/4 cup of milk. Add the flour mixture all at once, stirring only until moistened. Spoon onto tops of blackberry mixture in dollops. Do not try to cover the berries completely. Bake in a preheated 400° oven for about 40 minutes or until top is lightly browned. Serve warm with cream. Serves 6.

Tea Friends

SANDY SHELBY

In the first printing of *Midwestern Tea Room Pleasures*, I featured Sandy Shelby's Victorian Special Teas in Lynnwood, Illinois. Her teas were non-for-profit, monthly, theme teas that she held in her home for approximately 25 people. I have experienced some of my most memorable tea moments around Sandy's tea table. It was through those experiences that I learned most about the spiritual and psychological benefits of the private afternoon tea party.

Sandy's teas quickly turned into a tea ministry. That wasn't her intent; but quickly the Lord revealed to her that hospitality is her gift—a gift that needs to be shared. She has received so many testimonies from guests who have said that her teas touched their lives in positive ways. Alas, it appears that Sandy may no longer be able to continue with her teas because of the changes going on in her life. But she tells me that she strongly feels that her work with tea is not finished. I can't wait to see what comes next!

BIRD NESTS

8 ounces of chocolate chips
approximately 4 portions of Shredded Wheat cereal (not the bite-sized)

Melt the chocolate chips over a double boiler or in the microwave (stir often to prevent burning). Crush the cereal partially (not so that it becomes sawdust-like) Pour melted chips over the cereal and stir to coat. Drop the mixture by heaping teaspoonfuls onto a waxed paper covered baking sheet. The shapes can be irregular and approximately 1 1/2 inches in diameter. Indent a space in the center of each cereal mound to create a nest. Drop in 3 pastel, mini jelly beans. Chill to set. Makes approximately 20 nests.

♣ Sandy says that this easy recipe is perfect for a Spring, Easter, or nature themed tea. She is a big fan of easy, quick recipes.

ALLENE TURNBO

Allene has a fantastic gift shop in Lemont, Illinois, called *Neena's Treasures for all Seasons*. Hospitality is one of Allene's specialties. She carries a wide variety of gourmet foods including crackers and preserves perfect for these treats and, of course, teas. Lemont is a historic canal town that has many antique shops. It's about 30 miles southwest of Chicago.

JEZEBEL CRACKERS

Crackers (your choice but something rather plain)
Spreadable or softened cream cheese
Strawberry preserves
Cayenne pepper

Spread the crackers with cream cheese. Top the cream cheese with a layer of strawberry preserves. Sprinkle with cayenne pepper.

These would make a good alternative to tea sandwiches—so easy and plenty of zip!

Joyce Decherd
P.O. Box 787
Moline, IL 61266-0787

Please send me _____ copies of *Midwestern Tea Room Pleasures*.
@ $14.95 ea _____

Iowa residents add $.90 tax _____
Illinois residents add $.94 tax _____
Plus postage & handling @ $3.00 per book _____
Total $_____

Enclose check or money order
Make checks payable to Joyce Decherd.

Name _____
Address _____
City _____ State _____ Zip _____

Joyce Decherd
P.O. Box 787
Moline, IL 61266-0787

Please send me _____ copies of *Midwestern Tea Room Pleasures*.
@ $14.95 ea _____

Iowa residents add $.90 tax _____
Illinois residents add applicable tax _____
Plus postage & handling @ $3.00 per book _____
Total $_____

Enclose check or money order
Make checks payable to Joyce Decherd.

Name _____
Address _____
City _____ State _____ Zip _____